BAD BEHAVIOUR

Bad Behaviour

AN ANTHOLOGY OF ATROCIOUSNESS

Edited by Guy Philipps
Illustrated by William Rushton

Elm Tree Books
LONDON

Published by the Penguin Group
27 Wrights Lane, London W8 5TZ, England
Viking Penguin Inc, 40 West 23rd Street, New York,
New York 10010, U.S.A.
Penguin Books Australia Ltd, Ringwood, Victoria, Australia
Penguin Books Canada Ltd, 2801 John Street, Markham,
Ontario, Canada L3R 1B4
Penguin Books (N.Z.) Ltd, 182-190 Wairau Road, Auckland 10,
New Zealand

Penguin Books Ltd, Registered Offices: Harmondsworth,
Middlesex, England

First published in Great Britain 1988 by
Elm Tree Books

Copyright © 1988 by Toucan Books Limited

All rights reserved. Without limiting the rights under copyright
reserved above, no part of this publication may be reproduced,
stored in or introduced into a retrieval system or transmitted,
in any form or by any means (electronic, mechanical,
photocopying, recording or otherwise), without the prior
written permission of both the copyright owner and the above
publisher of this book.

British Library Cataloguing in Publication Data

Philipps, Guy
Bad Behaviour.
I. Title
828'.91407

ISBN 0-241-12484-0

Printed by Richard Clay Ltd,
Bungay, Suffolk

'God created the world,
but it is the Devil who keeps it going'

TRISTAN BERNARD

ACKNOWLEDGMENTS

My thanks to all those who have given permission to quote from works still in copyright, with apologies to any copyright holders who may inadvertently have been overlooked; I should be delighted to make amends in future editions. There is a list of sources quoted at the end of the book.

I should also like to thank everyone who has offered help and suggestions, and in particular William Boyd, Fram Dinshaw, Linda Kelly, Adam Nicolson, Nigel Nicolson, John Julius Norwich, Mollie Philipps, David Sexton and Xa Sturgis.

The book is dedicated to Rebecca, with love.

INTRODUCTION

When I was young, and still thought to be capable of virtue, I was given an Anthology of Goodness. Edited by a distinguished literary figure and Good Man, it consisted of a seemingly unending number of sayings and doings designed to improve and edify the youthful mind: handy for christenings, confirmations and other occasions for the ritual giving of faintly embarrassing presents.

Ever since I flung that book down in disgust I have felt that what the world really needed was an Anthology of Atrociousness. And so I got into the habit of filling a notebook with particularly admirable examples of bad behaviour. Here is a selection, a commonplace book of beastliness.

Bad behaviour has two essential qualities. It is deliberate, and it is enjoyable. That is all there is to it: this is a book about having fun by behaving abominably. The doer does what he does because it is enjoyable, and the more calculated the outrage, the greater the thrill. Only unfortunates whose lives were irredeemably ruined by that Anthology of Goodness will not know the rapture of badness, the exquisite joy, when the time and the place and, above all, the audience are right, of going too far.

Sometimes the villain, especially if he has a reputation to protect, may try to conceal his villainy. It is just possible that William Butler, said by Aubrey to have been 'the greatest Physitian of his time', meant only to cure his patients' suffering and not to enhance it:

'The Dr lyeing at the Savoy in London next the water side, where there was a Balcony look't into the Thames, a Patient came to him that was grievously tormented with an Ague. The Dr orders a boate to be in readinesse under his windowe, and discoursed with the patient (a

Gent.) in the Balcony, when, on a signal given, two or three lusty Fellowes came behind the Gentleman and threw him a matter of 20 feete into the Thames. This surprize absolutely cured him'

And even Longfellow was not sure how to take Queen Victoria's praise of HIAWATHA:

'The Queen said some kind things to him, and Longfellow replied that he was surprised to find himself so well known in England. "Oh, I assure you, Mr Longfellow," said the Queen, "you are very well known. All my servants read you."'

Usually, though, there is no doubt at all. Bad behaviour is a public pleasure, requiring an audience. Unlike most vices, it cannot be properly savoured in solitude. And if one is playing to the gallery, there is no point in mumbling one's lines or leaving the audience unsure what happened in the end.

Because the devil is so clearly enjoying his devilry, bad behaviour is enjoyable for the spectator as well. It is always nice to see some deserving soul giving himself a really good time. That is why there are no stories in this book of accidental misconduct. However catastrophic the consequences, the mere dropping of bricks is not bad behaviour. If the perpetrator is more humiliated than gleeful, the audience is likely to feel sympathy rather than the delight and secret envy that true naughtiness arouses; and that sympathy somehow takes away the zest that gives bad behaviour its unmistakable relish.

(Sympathy for the victim, though, does not even enter into the question. The interest in these stories is in the sinner and not the saint, in the lion, not the Christian. However shamefully he is treated, we do not care about the martyr's suffering. He is the straight man, only there to make up the numbers. These stories are funny because he is miserable. It is a sad reflection on human nature, but there it is.)

Bad behaviour is a simple enough notion, then. Yet the variations on the theme are infinite. Some motifs recur: there are quite a few bottoms, and there is enough wine-throwing in this book to make any modern advocate of the technique ashamed of her lack of originality. As a whole, though, the collection is a tribute to the breadth of human ingenuity and inventiveness.

The best bad behaviour is born of a spontaneous impulse. It cannot be premeditated or rehearsed. Of course, some great artists are constantly honing and developing their skills: George IV and Evelyn Waugh always stood head and shoulders above the mob. Few could live up to their standard. But for the majority, those who may just once or twice in their lives succumb to the magical temptation to go beyond the pale, the chance of badness comes without warning. The circumstances cannot be dictated, but they are there to be exploited. Even if it is only the most fleeting of opportunities, it is waiting to be seized.

Anyone may hear their particular destiny summoning them to greatness: I am especially proud of the two saints whose exploits are recorded in this collection. Although the famous and the powerful are well represented here, the book is also a monument to the unknowns who have taken their chance. Many of them names otherwise forgotten to history, their sole claim to the attention of posterity is that they once rose magnificently to a moment of outstanding badness.

The art of bad behaviour is, of course, of immemorial antiquity. The ability of the wicked to flourish like the green bay tree was a source of grievance to the Psalmist, and they have shown admirable perseverance ever since.

The great eras of abominableness, though, come and go. The thirty or forty years of the Prince Regent's leadership of society marked one glorious epoch, perhaps the greatest of all. It is as if latent wickedness was kindled at the mere approach of Prinny's magnificent person, inspiring his cronies to engage in competitive badness on a heroic scale. (My own favourite has always been Beau Brummell, as captured by Virginia Woolf:

'"Why, what could I do, my good fellow, but cut the connection? I discovered that Lady Mary actually ate cabbage!" – so he explained to a friend his failure to marry a lady.')

And while the nation's leaders outdid each other in atrociousness and indulged what their Victorian descendants despised as their moral turpitude, Britain defeated Napoleon and set out on world domination.

Something very similar had happened during the previous Golden Age of bad behaviour, the reign of Queen Elizabeth. The conjunction of national greatness and individual naughtiness is not mere coincidence. History demonstrates that the two go hand in hand: that is shown by the fact that since 1945 Britain has lost her position as the world's preeminently badly behaved nation. The great tradition has been taken up by the United States, where the torch lit by the English aristocracy has passed into the worthy hands of the democrats of the New World, the flames lovingly fanned by the heirs of Hemingway and Truman Capote.

This book, then, has educational value. Perhaps it may inspire a future national leader. For if anything emerges from these stories, it is that only those who understand and appreciate badness are fit to administer public affairs. At a time when every attempt to bring the atrociousness of the rich and powerful to the attention of an admiring public is met with a writ for libel, that is something to consider.

With the didactic quality of the work in mind, I have excluded fictional atrociousness from this collection. It is too easy for novelists or poets to make their characters behave appallingly. In Iris Murdoch's novel THE FLIGHT FROM THE ENCHANTER, for example, there is the following gem:

'Annette had never been in love, although she was not without experience. She had been deflowered at seventeen by a friend of her brother on the suggestion of the latter. Nicholas would have arranged it when she was sixteen, only he needed her just then for a black mass. "You must be rational about these things, Sis," he told her. "Don't build up an atmosphere of mystery and expectation, it'll only make you neurotic."'

It is too good to be true, and it is not as good as the stories that are true. I do not vouch for the veracity of every word in this book. None of it, though, seems remotely improbable.

So here it is, the Anthology of Atrociousness. It is likely to be of little use to the godparent or maiden aunt looking for something suitable to mark an occasion. It may be beneath the dignity of those who insist on looking at the stars; but I hope it will be a useful guide for the rest of us, who prefer, by concentrating on the gutter, to see what we are about to tread in.

Guy Philipps
MARCH 1988

The 17th. century antiquary Thomas Woodcock describes the bad behaviour of a learned contemporary:

Of Dr Thomas Goodwin, when ffellow of Catherine Hall. – He was somewhat whimsycall, in a frolick pist once in old Mr Lothian's pocket (this I suppose was before his trouble of conscience and conversion made him serious).

Postscript to a letter from Ann Fleming to Evelyn Waugh, 30 June 1958:

WHEN little Margaret [Waugh] grows up do *not* behave like John Barrymore did with his daughter Diana. John Barrymore who was sitting with Errol Flynn said as Diana passed by "Ever f-d her?" Errol Flynn had, but as the girl was sixteen, he thought it wise to show surprise and denial – "Don't miss it," said Barrymore, "she's terrific."

Barrymore's stage appearances fully lived up to his family life. The opening night in London in 1905 of THE DICTATOR, *starring Willie Collier, produced a memorable performance:*

THE first entrance of the wireless operator was important for a proper understanding of the play. The business provided that Jack [Barrymore] give Collier a wireless despatch written on two long sheets of paper. Collier would read the report aloud, thus advising the audience of the why, when, and wherefore of the action.

Jack appeared on cue, but had in his hand only a small fragment torn from a menu card, a triangle about the size of a Cape of Good Hope postage stamp. He offered this tiny absurdity to the astounded Collier with the usual dialogue, "Here, Chief, is the despatch."

Collier, his eye upon the scrap of paper, improvised, "But where is the real despatch? The longer one?"

Jack also improvised, "Here it is, sir. Or have your eyes gone back on you again?"

"Go to the wireless room", said the desperate Collier, "and bring the *first* despatch. There are two sheets of it. Remember? That's the one I want to read. Not a piece of confetti."

"But this *is* the first despatch", Jack insisted. "I took it down myself, word for word. Put on your bifocals." . . .

"Someone is trying to double-cross us. Go back and look again. I'm sure you will find the genuine message."

"But I *know* this is the one, sir", Jack insisted. "It was sent by a well-known female impersonator."

"Then have her, or him, send us another."

"But", Jack said, "he, or she, can't. He, or it, just died." He wiped away a tear, and sniffled, "Are you going to the funeral?"

"No", said Collier. "How can I?"

"Why not, sir?"

"Because", said Collier, "I haven't got a black dress!" He barked, "Now go for the other message." . . .

Jack went off-stage, leaving Collier to ad lib once again for almost half a minute. Then Barrymore re-appeared to present Collier with exactly the same triangular bit of paper!

"Sir, I have had this authenticated", and he held up the little scrap. "It was not written by the late female impersonator, but by the very clever fellow who engraves the Lord's Prayer on the heads of pins."

From Aubrey's BRIEF LIVES:

My old friend James Harrington, Esq., was well acquainted with Sir Benjamin Ruddyer, who was an acquaintance of Sir Walter Raleigh's. He told Mr. J.H. that Sir Walter Raleigh, being invited to dinner with some great person, where his son was to goe with him: He sayd to his Son, Thou art such a quarrelsome, affronting creature that I am ashamed to have such a Beare in my Company. Mr. Walt humbled himselfe to his Father, and promised he would behave himselfe mightily mannerly. So away they went, and Sir Benjamin, I thinke, with them. He sate next to his Father and was very demure at leaste halfe dinner time. Then sayd he, I this morning, not having the feare of God before my eies, but by the instigation of the devill, went to a Whore. I was very eager of her, kissed and embraced her, and went to enjoy her, but she thrust me from her, and vowed I should not, *For your father lay with me but an hower ago.* Sir Walt, being so strangely supprized and putt out of his countenance at so great a Table, gives his son a damned blow over the face; his son, as rude as he was, would not strike his father, but strikes over the face of the Gentleman that sate next to him, and sayed, *Box about, 'twill come to my Father anon.*

Anita Leslie, in EDWARDIANS IN LOVE, *describes the lengths to which her subjects would go to achieve their adulterous ends:*

Even the craftiest did not always succeed in his stratagems. Lord Charles Beresford (who was in love with Lady Warwick at the same time as the Prince of

Wales) told my grandfather that on one occasion he tiptoed into a dark room and jumped into the vast bed shouting "Cock-a-doodle-doo", to find himself, when trembling hands had lit a paraffin lamp, between the Bishop of Chester and his wife. The situation seemed very difficult to explain and he left the house before breakfast the next morning.

Horace Walpole, in his MEMOIRS OF THE REIGN OF GEORGE *tells the story of:*

LORD Anglesey, who beating his wife, she said, "How much happier is that wench (pointing to a housemaid) than I am!" He immediately kicked the maid down stairs, and then said, "Well! there is at least one grievance removed."

John Malcolm Brinnin describes in his memoir of Truman Capote how, when eating out with his lover, John O'Shea, the writer was besieged by autograph hunters.

"THERE was a time," said T., "when the only thing I'd be asked to autograph was a book. Now it's everything from gas station receipts to pricks." He turned to John. "Tell him what happened last night."

"We were at that backyard restaurant at the other end of the island," O'Shea began, "in a bar upstairs the owners sort of keep to themselves. The place was jammed with locals...maybe what you'd call the

BAD BEHAVIOUR

Lord Anglesey removes a grievance.

transient locals...like Jimmy Kirkwood and Peter Fonda and the usual clutch of game-fish machos roughing each other up for the benefit of those English queens down from Sugar Loaf or wherever it is they live, and things were pretty lively all round."...

"Anyway," said John, "up to our tables comes this chick ...not bad, but full of gush, who turns around, flips up a miniskirt and asks Truman to autograph her buns. Not batting an eyelash, he takes out a felt-tipped pen and scrawls his name across a plump little buttock. It was funny, really sort of nice. Then, not two minutes later, comes this kid bartender, Joey, they call him, who's obviously been eyeing the proceedings. The thing is , he's got his jockey shorts in his hand and not where they should be. One quick cruise and – everybody's listening now – I turn to Truman. 'You can't sign your name on *that*,' I said, 'but maybe you could in*iti*al it.'"

From Augustus Hare's journal, August 30, 1876:

TO-DAY the Duchess [the Dowager Duchess of Cleveland] has been talking much of the wicked Duchess of Gordon, her ancestress. She married all her daughters to drunken Dukes. One of them had been intended to marry Lord Brome, but his father, Lord Cornwallis, objected on account of the insanity in the Gordon family. The Duchess sent for him. "I understand that you object to my daughter marrying your son on account of the insanity in the Gordon family: now I can solemnly assure you that there is not a single drop of Gordon blood in her veins."

*Boswell and Dr Johnson dine at General Oglethorpe's,
April 10 1772:*

THE General told us, that when he was a very young man, I think only fifteen, serving under Prince Eugene of Savoy, he was sitting in a company at table with a Prince of Wirtemberg. The Prince took up a glass of wine, and, by a fillip, made some of it fly in Oglethorpe's face. Here was a nice dilemma. To have challenged him instantly, might have fixed a quarrelsome character upon the young soldier: to have taken no notice of it, might have been considered as cowardice. Oglethorpe, therefore, keeping his eye upon the Prince, and smiling all the time, as if he took what his Highness had done in jest, said *"Mon Prince,—"* (I forget the French words he used, the purport however was,) "That's a good joke; but we do it much better in England;" and threw a whole glass of wine in the Prince's face.

James Fox describes in WHITE MISCHIEF *the delights of the life led by rich English settlers in Kenya's 'Happy Valley' between the wars, where, according to Sir Derek Erskine, one of the survivors, 'cocaine was taken like snuff'. At a dinner party for the Prince of Wales in 1928, Erskine saw one of the guests manhandling another out of the room.*

WHEN Erskine asked what had happened, he was told, "Well, there is a limit, even in Kenya, and when someone offers cocaine to the Heir to the Throne, something has to be done about it, particularly when it is between courses at the dinner table."

Recording the sporting exploits of the Duke of Bedford, the SPORTING MAGAZINE *reported that in 1788 Lord Barrymore*

BETTED his Grace £500 to £400 that he produced a man who should eat a live cat, which was performed at the time appointed by a labouring man of Harpenden, near St Albans.

Cecil Beaton is reminded of the story of the Edwardian society figure Lady Bingham, stared at by a peculiar-looking stranger on a train:

LADY B's nervousness manifested itself by her bringing out her compact and making up her face which, of course, needed no such attention. She powdered liberally the parrot nose, rouged the lobster-malmaison cheeks, applied the brilliant lipstick, dusted the eyelids with blue, adjusted the spotted veil that swathed the turban trimmed with a firework display of cockfeathers. Lady Bingham once more threw a quick glance in the direction of the stranger. To her horror she heard him say: "Take off that veil." Lady Bingham, too terrified to pull the communication cord, or remonstrate in any way, obeyed the instruction. "Now take off that hat." With painted, trembling fingers Lady Bingham obeyed as the man's eyes continued to devour her. Lady Bingham, white as death under the rouge, did as she was bid. In fact, Lady Bingham permitted herself the humiliation of carrying out to the letter the madman's instructions to take off her overcoat, then her coat and waistcoat (she was wearing a smart *tailleur*), and now the blouse and

Bad Behaviour

A labouring man of Harpenden, near St Albans.

next the skirt, now the petticoat, now the camiknickers, now the corset, the brassière, and then the smart patent leather, high, red-heeled, buckled shoes. When the terrified nude was revealed in all her pearly beauty, the madman pointed aloft and commanded her to get up onto the luggage rack. With one arm closely guarding the communication cord, with the other the stranger helped the poor lady up into the required position. "Now don't move from there," the stranger commanded.

The train rushed on, past Andover, Basingstoke, on and on, louder and faster to Woking, while Lady Bingham lay on the rack with her admiring audience below. Each time Lady Bingham, during the hour and a half journey, wished to turn her body, her captor barked: "Don't move!" Lady B, frightened, cold and stiff, could only do as she was bid. At last the train drew into Vauxhall; the stranger had reached his destination. He leapt blithely to the platform, through the window blew a kiss of adieu to Lady Bingham, and vanished from sight.

Having discovered that his wife was having an affair with the Duke of York (afterwards James II), the Earl of Southesk determined to have his revenge. According to the contemporary MEMOIRS OF THE LIFE OF THE COUNT DE GRAMMONT,

He went to the *most infamous Places* to look for the *most infamous Disease*. He met with it, but yet was but half reveng'd: For, after he had gone through the *grand Remedy*, in order to get rid of it, his Lady did but restore him his *Present*, having no more Commerce with the Person for whom it was industriously prepar'd.

BAD BEHAVIOUR

Fearful, perhaps, of the wrath of his King, Thomas Cranmer, Archbishop of Canterbury under Henry VIII, concealed the fact of his second marriage for seventeen years. The lengths to which he was said to have gone to preserve his secret were noted by his contemporary Nicholas Harpsfield, who recorded in his TREATISE ON THE PRETENDED DIVORCE BETWEEN HENRY VIII. AND CATHARINE OF ARAGON *that Cranmer*

KEPT his woman very close, and sometime carried her about with him in a great chest full of holes, that his pretty nobsey might take breath at.

Fifty years later Robert Parsons developed the story in A TREATISE OF THREE CONVERSIONS OF ENGLAND *(1603), telling how Cranmer's bad behaviour was ultimately detected:*

SOONE after his being Archbishopp though he were a Priest, and had made a vow of chastity, yet got he a woman and carryed her about with him in a chest, when he had occasion to remove. Whereof ensued a strange chance at one tyme. For that carryinge downe his said chest among other of his furniture, when he went from London to Canterbury: yt happened, that at *Graves-End* (where the B[ishop] lay one night) his chests were brought a land, & put in a gallery. And this amonge other being much recomended to the shipmen, (as conteyning pretious stuffe belonging to my Lords grace) they severed yt from the rest, and putt yt up endlonge against the wall in my Lords chamber, with the womans head downeward, which putting her in ieopardy to breake her necke, she was forced at length to cry out. And so the chamberlyns perceaving the error, tooke her forth fowly disfigured, and as good as halfe dead. This is a most certayne story.

Edith Sitwell remembers Lord Strachey:

HE wasted no words in conversation. A young and robust friend of ours, Constant Lambert, meeting him at a party, said "you don't remember, Mr. Strachey? We met four years ago."
"Quite a nice interval, I think, don't you?" remarked Mr. Strachey pleasantly, and passed on.

Horace Walpole describes the behaviour of the Duke of Newcastle at the funeral of George II in November 1760:

HE fell into a fit of crying the moment he came into the chapel and flung himself back in a stall, the Archbishop hovering over him with a smelling bottle – but in two minutes his curiosity got the better of his hypocrisy and he ran about the chapel with his glass to spy who was or was not there, spying with one hand and mopping his eyes with t'other. Then returned the fear of catching cold, and the Duke of Cumberland, who was sinking with heat, felt himself weighed down, and turning round, found it was the Duke of Newcastle standing upon his train to avoid the chill of the marble.

From the Common-Place Book of Charles Phelps, an 18th-century Vicar of South Lynn:

DR J-k-n was Fellow of Magdalen in Oxford, and went frequently to Abington, a market-town 5 miles off; was a good customer to the landlady at the Red-Lion, and brought others that spent their money freely. But, as time went on, he was pretty deep in her debt, and she by dunning him made the debt a matter of talk. In this state of resentment, on his part, for the publication of his slackness of pay, he went to Abington one day, resolved to pay the debt. The landlady was gone out to a lying-in visit, in her best clothes, and had left her common apparel in a chamber adjoining to the dining room. J-n saw them, dressed himself in them, and then opened a sash-window and stood shewing his bare backside at the window to all the town, who took it and reported it to be the landlady's. 1757.

Daphne Fielding's autobiography, MERCURY PRESIDES, *begins:*

I have been told by people who knew my father and mother when they were first married that their quarrels were so violent that, after exhausting every throwable object in the room, they would use the baby as a missile. I was the baby.

Christopher Hibbert in his EDWARD VII: A PORTRAIT *retraces the steps of the then Prince of Wales through the brothels of Paris:*

HE had gone to the Maison Dorée with the Duc de Gramont to meet degenerate, passionate and

Bad Behaviour

The Prince of Wales enjoys Giulia Beneni's best side.

consumptive Giulia Beneni, known as La Barucci who arrived very late and, on being reprimanded by the Duke, turned her back on her royal visitor, lifted her skirts to her waist and said, "you told me to show him my best side".

Charles Osborne describes how the young W. H. Auden, when invited to the homes of his friends, 'would usually make an effort to behave with conventional politeness':

Rex Warner's parents thought Auden had charming manners: that he was given to raiding their pantry in the middle of the night, or that he took down the curtains in the bedroom and used them as blankets, was tactfully ignored. When he stayed with the Carritts, he removed their stair-carpet, still in search of nocturnal warmth, and placed it on his bed. He always got on well with Mrs Carritt, even though at breakfast on the first morning he tasted his tea and then said flatly, "Mrs Carritt, this tea is like tepid piss." He also hated the porridge Mrs Carritt served, and once vomited up his breakfast all over the geraniums in the front garden of the local post office, apologizing by going inside and announcing to the postmistress, "I'm sorry, madam, but it's the Carritts' porridge."

From Evelyn Waugh's diary, 8 December 1924:

I am at the moment just recovering from a very heavy bout of drinking. On the evening of the last day about which I have written I had a good drinking evening with

Alec, Terence, and Richard Greene. Exactly a week later I suddenly went to Oxford by the most impossible train which stopped at every station. I arrived at 10.30 and drove to 31 St. Aldate's where I found an enormous orgy in progress. Billy and I unearthed a strap and whipped Tony. Everyone was hideously drunk except strangely enough myself. Next day I moved to 40 Beaumont Street and began a vastly expensive career of alcohol. After a quiet day in cinemas, I had a dinner party of Claud, Elmley, Terence, Roger Hollis and a poor drunk called Macgregor. I arrived quite blind after a great number of cocktails at the George with Claud. Eventually the dinner broke up and Claud, Roger Hollis and I went off for a pub-crawl which after sundry indecorous adventures ended up at the Hypocrites where another blind was going on. Poor Mr Macgregor turned up after having lain with a woman but almost immediately fell backwards downstairs. I think he was killed. Next day I drank all the morning from pub to pub and invited to lunch with me at the New Reform John Sutro, Roger Hollis, Claud and Alfred Duggan. I am not sure if there was anyone else. I ate no lunch but drank solidly and was soon in the middle of a bitter quarrel with the president – a preposterous person called Cotts – who expelled me from the club. Alfred and I then drank double brandies until I could not walk. He carried me to Worcester where I fell out of a window and then relapsed into unconsciousness punctuated with severe but well-directed vomitings. I dined four times at various places and went to a drunk party at Worcester in someone's rooms I did not know.

BAD BEHAVIOUR

Lord Hervey describes a typical evening at the Court of George II:

His Majesty stayed about five minutes in the gallery; snubbed the Queen, who was drinking chocolate, for being always stuffing, the Princess Emily for not hearing him, the Princess Caroline for being grown fat, the Duke for standing awkwardly, Lord Hervey for not knowing what relation the Prince of Sultzbach was to the Elector Palatine, and then carried the Queen to walk, and be resnubbed, in the garden.

In the manuscript version of his bitterly hostile Dedication of DON JUAN *to the Poet Laureate, Robert Southey, Lord Byron wrote (of Milton): Would he subside into a hackney Laureat? A scribbling self-sold soul-hired scorned Iscariot' – under which the poet wrote this note:*

I doubt if Laureat & Iscariot be good rhymes but must say as Ben Johnson did to Sylvester who challenged him to rhyme with
"I, John Sylvester
"Lay with your Sister
Johnson answered – "I Ben Johnson lay with your wife"
Sylvester answered "that is not *rhyme*" – *no* Said Ben Johnson; "But it is *true.*"

Rupert Brooke and the 'Pagans' liked to pretend to be Noble Savages in Grantchester. In 1909 Virginia Woolf went to stay with him there. According to his latest biographer:

THE climax of the visit, if legend be true, came when he got her to bathe naked at Byron's Pool and showed off his party trick – jumping in and emerging with an instant erection. Virginia, who prided herself on knowledge of earth closets and 'the female inside', presumably took it in her stride.

Osbert Sitwell in his autobiography described his father, Sir George, in the full flower of his eccentricity:

LATTERLY he had coined several new slogans to express his individual sentiments, at last developed to their utmost capacity, and when, having risen from his bed to come down after dinner, he sat by himself, in full evening dress, white tie and waistcoat, in the ballroom in the middle of his Regency sofa, very long, and supported by a carved and painted lion at either end, so that he resembled a Byzantine Emperor on his throne, he would often at this hour, and always to the delight of his children, enunciate his favourite command disguised as a request:

"*I must ask anyone entering the house never to contradict me or differ from me in any way, as it interferes with the functioning of the gastric juices and prevents my sleeping at night.*"

BAD BEHAVIOUR

Rupert shows Virginia his party trick.

Bad Behaviour

Lady Mary Wortley Montagu writes to her sister, Lady Mar, 23 June 1727:

I can't tell whither you know a Tall, musical, silly, ugly thing, niece to Lady Essex Roberts, who is call'd Miss Leigh. She went a few days ago to visit Mrs. Betty Titchburne, Lady Sunderland's sister, who lives in the House with her, and was deny'd at the door; but with the true manners of a great Fool told the porter that if his Lady was at home she was very positive she would be very glad to see her. Upon which she was shew'd up stairs to Miss Titchburne, who was ready to drop down at the sight of her, and could not help asking her in a grave way how she got in, being deny'd to every mortal, intending to pass the Evening in devout preparations. Miss Liegh (sic) said she had sent away her chair and servants with intent of staying till 9 o'clock. There was then no Remedy and she was ask'd to sit down, but had not been there a quarter of an hour when she heard a violent rap at the door, and somebody vehemently run up stairs. Miss Titchburne seem'd much surprizd and said she beleiv'd it was Mr. Edgcombe, and was quite amaz'd how he took it into his Head to visit her. During these Excuses, enter Edgcombe, who appear'd frighted at the sight of a third person. Miss Titchburne told him almost at his Entrance that the Lady he saw there was a perfect mistriss of music, and as he passionately lov'd it she thought she could not oblige him more than by desiring her to play. Miss Leigh very willingly sat to the Harpsicord, upon which her Audience decamp'd to the Bed Chamber, and left her to play over 3 or 4 lessons to her selfe. They return'd and made what excuses they could, but said very frankly they had not heard her performance and begg'd her to begin again, which she comply'd with, and gave them the opertunity of a second retirement. Miss Leigh was by this time all Fire and

Flame to see her heavenly Harmony thus slighted, and when they return'd told them she did not understand playing to an empty room. Mr. Edgcombe begg'd ten thousand pardons, and said if she would play Godi, it was a Tune he dy'd to hear, and it would be an Obligation he should never forget. She made answer, she would do him a much greater Obligation by her Absence, which she suppos'd was all that was wanting at that Time, and run downstairs in a great Fury, to publish as fast as she could, and was so indefatigable in this pious design that in 4 and twenty hours all the people in Town had heard the story, and poor Edgcombe met with nothing where ever he went but complements about his third Tune, which is reckon'd very handsome in a Lover past forty.

The contemporary biographer of St. Hugh of Lincoln describes the saint's extraordinary devotion to holy relics when Bishop of Lincoln:

WHEN he was at the celebrated monastery of Fécamp, he extracted by biting two small fragments of the bone of the arm of the most blessed lover of Christ, Mary Magdalen. This bone had never been seen divested of its wrappings by the abbot or any of the monks who were present on that occasion, for it was sewn very tightly into three cloths, two of silk and one of ordinary linen. They did not dare to accede even to the bishop's prayer to be allowed to see it. He, however, taking a small knife from one of his notaries, hurriedly cut the thread and undid the wrappings. After reverently examining and kissing the much venerated bone, he tried unsuccessfully to break it with his fingers, and then bit it first with his incisors and finally with his molars. By this means he broke off two fragments, which he handed immediately to the writer.

BAD BEHAVIOUR

The Earl of Clarendon, Governor of New York and
New Jersey, represents Queen Anne
as faithfully as possible.

BAD BEHAVIOUR

Lord Glenbervie notes in his diary a conversation with Horace Walpole (Lord Orford) about Edward Hyde, third Earl of Clarendon, Governor of New York and New Jersey from 1701 to 1708:

He was a clever man. His great insanity was dressing himself as a woman. Lord Orford says that when Governor in America he opened the Assembly dressed in that fashion. When some of those about him remonstrated, his reply was, "You are very stupid not to see the propriety of it. In this place and particularly on this occasion I represent a woman (Queen Anne) and ought in all respects to represent her as faithfully as I can."

From John Taylor's RECORDS OF MY LIFE *(1832):*

A relation of her grace [the Duchess of Marlborough] of an eccentric character, and who was commonly called Jack Spencer, used always to pay his respects to her on her birth-day. On one occasion he went in a chairman's coat, which he threw off in her presence, and appeared naked. Her grace remonstrated with him on such a shameless appearance. "Shameless!" said he, "why I am in my *birth-day suit.*"

From Cecil Beaton's diary, 1949:

I wonder if Evelyn [Waugh] ever really likes anybody? I believe his second marriage to be an exceptionally happy one, but I cannot imagine his ever loving anyone. Diana [Cooper] says she loves him though she is fully conscious of the unkind and cruel things he does to people. Once the two of them were motoring together through Marlborough. At some traffic lights they came to a stop, and an anguished pedestrian put his head through the car window and said: "I've got a train to catch. Can you tell me the way to the railway station?" Evelyn gave him elaborate instructions. The man ran up the hill in a muck sweat. Diana put her foot on the accelerator.

"How clever of you to know where the station is."

"I don't," said Evelyn. "I always give people the wrong directions."

The pre-eminent 18th-century classical scholar Richard Porson summarises a tour of European centres of learning:

I went to Frankfort, and got drunk
With that most learn'd Professor Brunck:
I went to Worts, and got more drunken,
With that more learn'd Professor Runcken.

The Oxford don Nevill Coghill had the privilege of teaching W. H. Auden English.

ONE day, Coghill arrived late for a tutorial to find Auden already there, sitting at his tutor's desk and reading his letters with an air of great concentration. Looking up, Auden said, "Ah, you're here. Good. What have you done with the second page of this letter?"

From the MÉMOIRES SECRETS *of de Bachaumont, 25 July 1772:*

THE news from Marseilles is that M. le Comte de Sade, who caused such a stir in 1768 by the lunatic horrors which he inflicted on a girl...has just provided in this town a spectacle, pleasant at first, but appalling in its consequences. He gave a ball, to which a large number of guests were invited. Into the pudding course he inserted some chocolates so delicious that several people ate them. There were plenty of these, and nobody went short, but in them he had inserted 'Spanish Fly'. The virtue of this preparation is well known; and, as it turned out, all those who had eaten it, burning with unchaste desire, gave themselves up to all the excesses to which the most lascivious frenzy can carry one. The ball degenerated into one of those licentious parties renowned among the Romans. The most modest women could not do enough to give expression to the itch which had seized them. Thus M. de Sade enjoyed the sister-in-law with whom he has fled to preserve himself from the penalty which he deserves. Several persons are dead from the excesses to which they gave themselves up in their Priapic fury and others are still severely indisposed.

Sir William Fraser, a close friend of the Victorian novelist and Cabinet Minister Lord Lytton, told in HIC ET UBIQUE *how*

TRAVELLING in Italy, I remember that the train was passing Dezenzano, on the Lago di Garda at the time, a lady and gentleman were in the carriage with me: I was reading one of Lord Lytton's novels in the Tauchnitz edition; the gentleman said to me "I can tell you a very remarkable story of Lord Lytton." He kept his word: "I must tell you that I was solicitor to Lady Lytton in the difficulties which continued between her and her husband. Not long after their marriage Mr and Mrs Lytton Bulwer, as they then were, were travelling in an open carriage along the Riviera, between Genoa and Spezzia; Lord Lytton was dressed in the somewhat fantastic costume which at that period he affected. The vetturino drove. Mrs Bulwer's maid was sitting beside him: the happy couple were in an open carriage. Passing through one of the many villages close to the sea, they observed a singularly handsome girl standing at a cottage door. Mr Bulwer, with somewhat ill-advised complacency, turning to his wife, said 'Did you notice how that girl looked at me?' The lady, with an acidity which developed itself later in life, replied 'The girl was not looking at you in admiration: if you wear that ridiculous dress no wonder people stare at you.' The bridegroom thereupon with an admirable sense of Logic said 'You think that people stare at my dress; and not at me: I will give you the most absolute and convincing proof that your theory has no foundation.' He then proceeded to divest himself of every particle of clothing except his hat and boots: and taking the place of the lady's maid drove for ten miles in this normal condition."

Ralph Nevill, in Sporting Days and Sporting Ways *lists some of the 'eccentricities' of the notorious 'Mad Marquis' of Waterford:*

He painted the Melton toll-bar a bright red, put aniseed on the hoofs of a parson's horse, and hunted the terrified divine with bloodhounds. On another occasion he put a donkey into the bed of a stranger at an inn. He took a hunting-box in the shires, and amused himself with shooting out the eyes of the family portraits with a pistol. He smashed a very valuable French clock on the staircase at Crockford's with a blow of his fist, and solemnly proposed to one of the first railway companies in Ireland to start two engines in opposite directions on the same line in order that he might witness the smash, for which he proposed to pay.

BAD BEHAVIOUR

The Mad Marquis has fun at Crockford's.

Bad Behaviour

The 18th-century Irish writer Dorothea Herbert recalled in her Retrospections of an Outcast *the antics of her cousins Ned Eyre and his sister, Mrs White,*

As once at Cork when he promised to paint the Cheeks of a very pale Lady for an assembly – When she came down dressed to the Parlour, He at one side and Mrs White at the other scrubb'd her Cheeks – one with the deepest Crimson the other with plain Wool, and then hurried her off without letting her go to the Glass – For fear the Joke should light all on their pale friend, and her odd Cheeks of Various Hue – The Brother and Sister carried Jalap [a powerful purgative] in their pockets which they secretly mix'd with the Tea and Coffee – So that the Ladies and Gentlemen of the Ball Room soon found something else to think of besides laughing at Ned Eyre's pale protegee – The worthy Pair locked the Ball Room Door and a General Confusion ensued – Some were fainting Some weeping whilst their wicked Physicians escaped and dröve home.

From Dorothea Herbert's account in Retrospections of an Outcast *of her cousin Mrs White:*

At the Age of fourteen Mrs White then Miss Eyre was devoutly carried to a Confirmation, but was so vex'd at being forced to take all her Sins on herself that She stuck her Head full of Iron Pins with the Points up to annoy the Bishop who was terribly scratched and torn when he laid his hands on his Contumelious Disciple.

In his autobiography, A BETTER CLASS OF PERSON, *the playwright John Osborne describes his mounting irritation during a winter repertory season in Scarborough with the disapproving fastidiousness of the actress Lynne Reid Banks. Osborne, however, had the last word:*

SOME time later at an improbably posh party in London I offered her a sandwich. I had taken some trouble to insert among the smoked salmon and cream cheese, like a worm in the bud, a used French letter. The unbelieving repulsion on her face, the prig struck by lightning, was fixed for ever for me, like Kean's Macbeth.

From the Rev. Benjamin Newton's diary, 20 July 1818:

WE arrive at Wensley where we found all the family well, about 1/2 past 2 and sat down at four to an excellent dinner and to an excellent story of my old friend about an acquaintance and I believe relative of his, the rector of Finchampstead in Essex, a man of fortune, who kept his coach and four and made his two sons postillion calling one son of a whore, whom he had by his wife who was his housekeeper before marriage, and the other son of a bitch whom he had by her afterwards.

From Aubrey's life of Sir (later Saint) Thomas More, Lord Chancellor under Henry VIII:

SIR William Roper, of Eltham, in Kent, came one morning, pretty early, to my Lord, with a proposall to marry one of his daughters. My Lord's daughters were then both together abed in a truckle-bed in their father's chamber asleep. He carries Sir William into the chamber and takes the Sheete by the corner and suddenly whippes it off. They lay on their Backs, and their smocks up as high as their arme-pitts. This awakened them, and immediately they turned on their bellies. Quoth Roper, I have seen both sides, and so gave a patt on the buttock, he made choice of, sayeing, Thou art mine. Here was all the trouble of the wooeing.

Having arrived late for an examination in Rudiments of Faith and Religion at Oxford, Oscar Wilde failed to show the contrition expected by the examiners, all learned men of the cloth, and led by Dr. Spooner, himself a nephew of the Archbishop of Canterbury. Wilde's contemporary Douglas Sladen witnessed the scene that followed:

THE examiners were so annoyed at his impertinence that they gave him a Bible, and told him to copy out the long twenty-seventh chapter of the Acts. He copied it out so industriously in his exquisite handwriting that their hearts relented, and they told him that he need not write out any more. Half-an-hour afterwards they noticed that he was copying it out as hard as ever, and they called him up to say, "Didn't you hear us tell you, Mr. Wilde, that you needn't copy out any more?"

"Oh yes," he said, "I heard you, but I was so interested in what I was copying, that I could not leave off. It was all about a man named Paul, who went on a voyage, and was caught in a terrible storm, and I was afraid that he would be drowned, but, do you know, Mr. Spooner, he was saved, and when I found he was saved, I thought of coming to tell you."

BAD BEHAVIOUR

According to the account of Douglas Ainslie (whose own knowledge of scripture seems to leave something to be desired), Wilde

WAS put on to construe from the Greek of the New Testament at the verse of St. Matthew which records the sale of the Saviour for thirty pieces of silver by Baraḅbas [*sic*]. Wilde, who got a First in Greats and taught Mrs. Langtry Latin, construed a few verses rapidly and correctly. The examiner interrupted: "Very good, that will do, Mr. Wilde." "Hush, hush", replied the candidate, raising an admonitory finger, "let us proceed and see what happened to the unfortunate man."

Lord Hervey was present at the deathbed of Queen Caroline, wife of George II, in 1737, and heard her dying wish, that her husband should marry again:

IT is not necessary to examine whether the Queen's reasoning was good or bad in wishing the King, in case she died, should marry again. It is certain she did wish it, had often said so when he was present, and when he was not present, and when she was in health, and gave it now as her advice to him when she was dying; upon which his sobs began to rise and his tears to fall with double vehemence. Whilst in the midst of this passion, wiping his eyes, and sobbing between every word, with much ado he got out this answer: "Non – j'aurai – des – maîtresses."

From Evelyn Waugh's diary, 6 March 1946:

AN offensive letter from a female American Catholic. I returned it to her husband with the note: "I shall be grateful if you will use whatever disciplinary means are customary in your country to restrain your wife from writing impertinent letters to men she does not know."

His friend and biographer Tom Moore noted in his journal numerous examples of the bad behaviour of the playwright and politician R.B. Sheridan. On 16 December 1820:

LORD John [Russell] told a good trick of Sheridan's upon Richardson – Sheridan had been driving 3 or 4 hours in a hackney coach, when, seeing Richardson pass, he hailed him, and made him get in – he instantly contrived to introduce a topic upon which Richardson (who was the very soul of disputatiousness) always differed with him – and, at last affecting to be mortified by R.'s arguments, said "You really are too bad – I cannot bear to listen to such things – I will not stay in the same coach with you" and accordingly got out & left him – Richardson hallooing out triumphantly after him "Ah, you're beaten – you're beaten" – nor was it till the heat of his victory had a little cooled that he found out he was left in the lurch to pay for Sheridan's three hours' coaching.

Somerset Maugham recalls the novelist Elizabeth von Arnim:

I asked Elizabeth once whether the story I had often heard was true that when her husband was very ill she read to him as he lay in bed the book in which she had drawn a caustic portrait of him. When she reached the last page, so the story ran, shattered by what he had been made to listen to, he turned his face to the wall and died. She looked at me blandly and said:

"He was very ill. He would have died in any case."

Bad Behaviour

From Oscar Wilde's 'Pen, Pencil, and Poison', a study of Thomas Wainewright, aesthete and murderer:

When a friend reproached him with the murder of Helen Abercrombie [his sister-in-law] he shrugged his shoulders and said, "Yes; it was a dreadful thing to do, but she had very thick ankles."

Sir John Harington describes to Mr. Secretary Barlow a masque representing the visit of the Queen of Sheba to Solomon, arranged to honour the visit of the King of Denmark to the Court of James I in 1606:

Alass! as all earthly thinges do fail to poor mortals in enjoyment, so did prove our presentment hereof. The Lady who did play the Queens part did carry most precious gifts to both their Majesties; but, forgetting the steppes arising to the canopy, overset her caskets into his Danish Majesties lap, and fell at his feet, tho I rather think it was in his face. Much was the hurry and confusion; cloths and napkins were at hand to make all clean. His Majesty then got up and woud dance with the Queen of Sheba; but he fell down and humbled himself before her, and was carried to an inner chamber and laid on a bed of state; which was not a little defiled with the presents of the Queen which had been bestowed on his garments; such as wine, cream, jelly, beverage, cakes, spices, and other good matters. The entertainment and show went forward, and most of the presenters went backward, or fell down, wine did so occupy their upper chambers. Now did appear, in rich dress, Hope, Faith, and Charity: Hope did assay to speak, but wine rendered her endeavours so feeble that she withdrew, and hoped the King would excuse her brevity. Faith was then all alone, for I am certain she was not joyned with good works; and left the Court in a staggering condition. Charity came to the Kings feet, and seemed to cover the multitude of sins her sisters had committed: In some sorte she made obeysance and brought giftes, but said she would return home again, as there was no gift which heaven had not already given his Majesty; she then returned to Hope and Faith, who were both sick and spewing in the lower hall. Next came *Victory*, in bright armour, and presented a rich sword to the King, who did not accept it, but put it by with his hand; and, by a strange medley of versification, did endeavour to make suit to the King; but Victory did not tryumph long, for, after much lamentable utterance, she was led away like a silly captive, and laid to sleep in the outer steps of the anti-chamber. Now did Peace make entry, and strive to get formoste to the King; but I grieve to tell how great wrath she did discover unto those of her attendants, and, much contrary to her own semblance, most rudely made war with her olive branch, and laid on the pates of those who did oppose her coming.'

The seventeeth century astrologer William Lilly described in his autobiographical HISTORY OF HIS LIFE AND TIMES *a fellow 'nibbler at astrology', one William Poole:*

HE pretended to poetry; and that posterity may have a taste of it, you shall have here inserted two verses of his own making; the occasion of making them was thus. One Sir Thomas Jay, a Justice of the Peace in Rosemary-Lane, issued out his warrant for the apprehension of Poole, upon a pretended suggestion, that he was in

William Poole has his revenge.

company with some lewd people in a tavern, where a silver cup was lost, *Anglice* stolen. Poole, hearing of the warrant, packs up his little trunk of books, being all his library, and runs to Westminster; but hearing some months after that the Justice was dead and buried, he came and enquired where the grave was; and after the discharge of his belly upon the grave, left these two verses upon it, which he swore he made himself.

Here lieth buried Sir Thomas Jay, Knight,
Who being dead, I upon his grave did shite.

It was said of John Christie, the founder of the Glyndebourne Festival Opera, that he 'was not above using his distinguished position to indulge a schoolboy sense of fun.'

SITTING next to the Queen at dinner one evening, he removed his glass eye and polished it for several minutes with his handkerchief. When he had finished, he popped it back, turned to the Queen and asked "In straight, Ma'am?"

From the diary of Dr. Edward Lake, chaplain and tutor to the Princesses Mary and Anne, daughters of the Duke of York (afterwards James II), brother of King Charles II:

October 21st, 1677 – The Duke of York din'd at Whitehall; after dinner return'd to Saint James', took Lady Mary into her closet, and told her of the marriage designed between her and the Prince of Orange; whereupon her highness wept all that afternoon and the following day...

Nov. 4th. – At nine o'clock at night the marriage was solemnised in her highness's bed-chamber. The King, who gave her away, was very pleasant all the while; for he desir'd that the bishop of London would make haste, lest his sister should be delivered of a son, and so the marriage be disappointed; and when the prince endowed her with all his worldly goods, he willed her to put all up in her pockett, for 'twas clear gains. At eleven o'clock they went to bed, and his majesty came and drew the curtains, and said to the prince, "Now, nephew, to your worke! Hey! St. George for England!"

According to Charlotte Elizabeth, Duchesse d'Orléans, writing from the Court of her brother-in-law Louis XIV, the behaviour of the bridegroom (soon to become King William III) was well up to the standard set by his uncle by marriage:

There is a great deal of talk about the Prince of Orange's wedding, and among other things it is said that he went to bed in woollen drawers on his wedding night. When the King of England suggested that he might care to take them off, he replied that since he and his wife would have to live together for a long time she would have to get used to his habits; he was accustomed to wearing his woollens, and had no intention of changing now.

After the tragically early death of his wife Elizabeth (Lizzie), the poet and artist Dante Gabriel Rossetti invited the novelist George Meredith and the poet A. C. Swinburne to share his house in Chelsea.

THE household which assembled at 16 Cheyne Walk in the autumn of 1862 might have been the ideal Pre-

Bad Behaviour

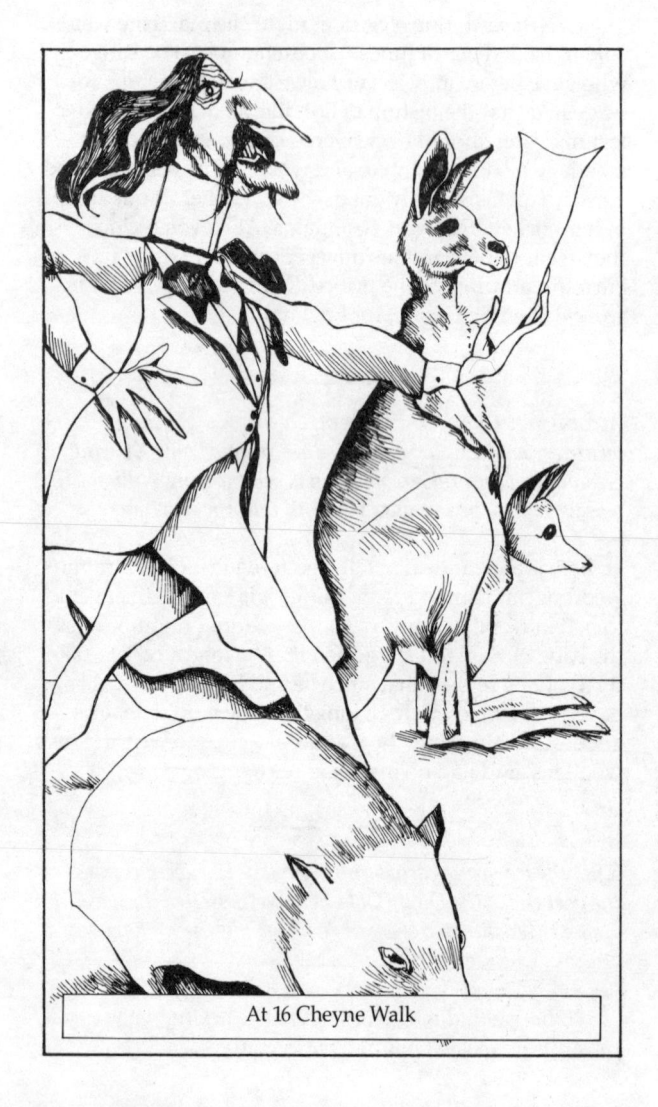

At 16 Cheyne Walk

Raphaelite, or perhaps Bohemian, community... Tudor House, as it was also known, was a sixteenth-century red-brick dwelling with gardens in which Rossetti was able to keep the pet animals of his collection, including a wombat, an armadillo and even a kangaroo. The house looked out across the foreshore of the Thames, with the raffish bustle of Cremorne Gardens a little way to the west... The visitors to Cheyne Walk included established artists like Frederick Leighton and younger men of promise like Whistler and Frederick Sandys. The arrangement promised comradeship and devotion to art.

The wombat ate the cigars. Meredith turned out to be wittier than the others and made fun of Rossetti in front of his guests. Rossetti threw a cup of tea in his face. Swinburne's nervous energy got on Rossetti's nerves, "dancing all over the studio like a wild cat", as Rossetti described him... Then things grew worse. Meredith was revolted by Rossetti's gargantuan breakfasts, bacon surrounded by a circle of eggs. Swinburne knocked Morris into a cupboard and smashed Rossetti's china. With a new acquaintance, Simeon Solomon, he romped naked about the house, sliding down the banisters and shrilly waking the echoes. Rossetti planned to accommodate his new mistress, Fanny Cornforth, whom Swinburne out of loyalty to Lizzie always referred to as "The Bitch". Meredith, driven to distraction by the row, swore that he "would certainly have kicked Swinburne downstairs had he not foreseen what a clatter his horrid little bottom would have made as it bounced from step to step."

Bad Behaviour

Relations between landlord and tenant were not always so strained. Sir Edmund Gosse, Swinburne's biographer, entrusted only to his unpublished 'Confidential Paper' on the poet's 'moral irregularities' the story of Rossetti's attempt to have Algernon relieved of his protracted virginity:

It was in the summer, I think, of 1867, that London went mad over the performance of a Miss Adah Isaacs Menken, who was carried round the stage in tights bound to the back of a very tame horse, as "Mazeppa". Her face was no longer particularly handsome, but she had a very fine figure. She was not much more than thirty, but she had been married many times, and now was dispensing with a husband. She was a strange mixture of coarseness and good-natured sensibility; she had lived with prize-fighters, and she wrote reams of lachrymose yearning poetry. It was agreed at Chelsea that she should be approached, and that she should be induced to take up the case of Algernon...Swinburne was taken to see her act in "Mazeppa", and her beauties were pointed out to him; it was further explained that she had a tremendous admiration for him. When his vanity was completely awakened, she paid him a visit, and according to his own account, then and there spent the night with him. She either lived altogether, or was a very frequent visitor, at his lodgings for some time, and they were very friendly indeed, but as Miss Menken apologetically observed to D.G.R., she "didn't know how it was, but she hadn't been able to get him up to the scratch", and so felt she must leave him...

In talking about Swinburne, she expressed vexation at having failed in the particular mission on which she had been employed, and naively remarked to Rossetti "I can't make him understand that *biting's* no use!"

Bad Behaviour

Dante Gabriel Rossetti anatomises Miss Menken for his virgin friend.

BAD BEHAVIOUR

William Lilly lists the charges he brought in 1642 against Isaac Antrobus, parson of Egremond, to have him deprived of his living:

   I. That Antrobus baptized a cock, and called him Peter.
   II. He had knowledge of such a woman and of her daughter, *viz.* of both their bodies, in as large a manner as ever of his own wife.
   III. Being drunk, a woman took a cord and tied it about his privy members unto a manger in a stable.
   IV. Being a continual drunkard.
   V. He never preached, &c.

Ian Fleming and the novelist Rosamond Lehmann were old friends, although her affection for him was not unwavering (she is said once to have thrown a dead octopus into his bedroom when annoyed.) But between her and his wife Ann, whom he married comparatively late in life, there was little love lost. After his marriage, Fleming asked Miss Lehmann to stay at Goldeneye, his house in Jamaica, as she had often done before. In his changed circumstances, however, it soon became clear that the invitation had been a mistake. Fleming decided that the only solution was for her to leave as soon as possible. According to Mark Amory, the editor of Ann Fleming's letters,

FLEMING appealed to Noël Coward to persuade her to stay with him instead and he agreed at a price, saying in front of her, "I'll settle for the Polaroid camera." Fleming handed it over, there was a pause and Coward added "And the tripod." He got that, too.

BAD BEHAVIOUR

James Harris, Earl of Malmesbury, undertook in April 1795 the introduction of the Prince of Wales (later George IV) to his bride-to-be, the less than beautiful Princess Caroline of Brunswick:

I, according to the established etiquette, introduced (no one else being in the room) the Princess Caroline to him. She very properly, in consequence of my saying it was the right mode of proceeding, attempted to kneel to him. He raised her (gracefully enough), and embraced her, said barely one word, turned round, retired to a distant part of the apartment, and calling me to him, said, "Harris, I am not well; pray get me a glass of brandy." I said, "Sir, had you not better have a glass of water?" – upon which he, much out of humour, said, with an oath, "No; I will go directly to the Queen," and away he went. The Princess, left during this short moment alone, was in a state of astonishment; and, on my joining her, said, "Mon Dieu! est ce que le Prince est toujours comme cela? Je le trouve très gros, et nullement aussi beau que son portrait."

After their inauspicious first meeting, the wedding of the Prince and Princess was, if anything, even less successful:

SHE approached the altar confidently and stood there chatting away to the Duke of Clarence with characteristic gusto as she awaited the arrival of the bridegroom. When he came, supported by the unmarried Dukes of Bedford and Roxburghe, he was seen to be extremely nervous and agitated. He had obviously been drinking; and at the beginning of the ceremony the Duke of Bedford, who had seen him swallow several glasses of brandy, had difficulty in preventing him from falling over... At one point he suddenly stood in the middle of a prayer. The Archbishop of Canterbury, John Moore, paused for a moment until the King stepped forward and whispered something to his son who then knelt down again...

After the ceremony the King and Queen held a Drawing-Room in the Queen's apartments to which the Prince conducted his bride almost in silence. The Duke of Leeds, who was walking in front of them, "could not help remarking how little conversation passed between them during the procession, and the coolness and indifference apparent in the manner of the Prince." When the Prince appeared in the Queen's apartments, so Lady Maria Stuart said, he looked "like death and full of confusion, as if he wished to hide himself from the looks of the whole world. I think," she added, "he is much to be pitied."...

The Prince's drunkenness increased as night approached, so his bride afterwards recounted; and when he did eventually make his way into her bedroom, he fell insensible into the fireplace where he remained all night and where she left him. In the morning he had recovered sufficiently to climb into bed with her.

Nor did matters ever improve. More than 25 years later, Henry Edward Fox recorded in his journal:

WHEN the news of Napoleon's death came, before the King had been informed of it by his Ministers, Sir E. Nagle, anxious to communicate the welcome tidings, said to him, "Sir, your bitterest enemy is dead". "Is she, by God!" said the tender husband.

After the death of Benjamin Jowett, Master of Balliol College since 1870, the OXFORD CHRONICLE *of 7th October, 1893 recorded:*

ONE day he and a pupil had taken a long walk together. At the offset, the undergraduate made various laudable efforts at starting subjects of conversation, but finding that they were received with absolutely no comment, or only an inarticulate little sound suggestive of nothing, he too relapsed into silence, which was maintained unbroken till the end of the walk, when with irrelevant geniality Mr Jowett remarked, "You must cultivate the art of conversation. Good morning!"

Augustus Hare tells of a similar incident in THE STORY OF MY LIFE:

I was profoundly grateful to Mr. Jowett, but being constantly asked to breakfast alone with him was a terrible ordeal. Sometimes he never spoke at all, and would only walk round the room looking at me with unperceiving, absent eyes as I ate my bread and butter, in a way that, for a very nervous boy, was utterly terrific. Walking with this kind and silent friend was even worse: he scarcely ever spoke, and if, in my shyness, I said something at one milestone, he would make no response at all until we reached the next, when he would say abruptly, "Your last observation was singularly commonplace," and relapse into silence again.

BAD BEHAVIOUR

The Fourth Duke of Ancaster and his favourite missile.

Horace Walpole discusses the will of the 4th Duke of Ancaster, who died in July 1779:

I hear he has left a legacy to a very small man that was always his companion, and whom, when he was drunk, he used to fling at the heads of the company, as others fling a bottle.

Jacqueline Susann, author of THE VALLEY OF THE DOLLS *and the pioneer of modern pulp fiction, was promoting her first blockbuster coast to coast when she momentarily lost America's attention:*

ABOUT a week after the publication of *Every Night, Josephine!* John F. Kennedy was assassinated. Shortly after, Jackie arrived at Berney Geis's office for a publicity meeting. She found the entire staff, like so many other Americans, clustered around a television set, watching the nonstop coverage from Texas in silent, stunned disbelief. She glanced at the television and blurted, "Why the fuck does this have to happen to me? This is gonna ruin my tour!"

The Oxford antiquary Anthony Wood noted a contemporary scandal, 'that notorious business in the balcony in the Strand at London', in his autobiographical THE LIFE AND TIMES OF ANTHONY WOOD *under June 1663:*

SIR Charles Sedley, Bt. somtimes of Wadham Coll., Charles lord Buckhurst (afterwards earl of Middlesex), Sir Thomas Ogle &c. were at a cook's house at the signe of the Cock in Bow-street neare Covent-Garden within the libertie of Westminster; and being all inflam'd with strong liquors, they went into the balcony joyning to their chamber-window, and putting downe their breeches, they excrementized in the street. Which being done Sedley stripped himself naked, and with eloquence preached blasphemy to the people.

Pepys recorded further details of this 'frollick' in his diary for 1 July 1663:

Thence by water with Sir W. Batten to Trinity-house, there to dine with him, which we did; and after dinner we fell in talking, Sir J. Mennes and Mr. Batten and I – Mr. Batten telling us of a late trial of Sir Charles Sydly the other day, before my Lord Chief Justice Foster and the whole Bench – for his debauchery a little while since at Oxford Kates; coming in open day into the Balcone and showed his nakedness – acting all the postures of lust and buggery that could be imagined, and abusing of scripture and, as it were, from thence preaching a Mountebanke sermon from that pulpitt, saying that there he hath to sell such a pouder as should make all the cunts in town run after him – a thousand people standing underneath to see and hear him. And that being done, he took a glass of wine and washed his prick in it and then drank it off; and then took another and drank the King's health.

According to Wood, at his trial

SIR Charles Sedley being fined 500*li*. he made answer, that he thought he was the first man that paid for shiting.

BAD BEHAVIOUR

LORD Glasgow, having flung a waiter through the window of his club, brusquely ordered: "Put him on the bill."

Lord Glenbervie recorded in his journal a story told him by a Miss Hotham:

SHE said that when Sir William Stanhope, in his old age, was about to marry Miss Delaval (I think she was sister to Sir Francis, Foote's friend) he went to inform his brother, the Earl of Chesterfield, of it. Lord Chesterfield joked with him on the likelihood that the marriage would not produce an heir to the family honours. "Why so?" said Sir William. *"You know, brother, I have a great many friends."*

This recalled to my memory the anecdote of Lady Anne Foley, which perhaps is already in one of these earlier volumes. Poor good-natured Ned Foley had also *many friends*, all the witty and wicked satellites of Charles Fox and *accompagnés de plusieurs autres*. Lady Anne a few days after one of her lyings-in wrote this short note and postscript to Fitzpatrick. "Dear Richard, I give you joy. I have just made you the father of a beautiful boy. Yours, etc. *P.S.* – This is not [a] circular."

Lord Holland gives Lord Macaulay an account of a visit he paid in 1792 to the Court of King Christian VII of Denmark:

ONE day the Neapolitan Ambassador came to the levee, and made a profound bow to his majesty. His majesty bowed still lower. The Neapolitan bowed down his head almost to the ground; – when behold! – The King clapped his hands on his excellency's shoulders and jumped over him like a boy playing at leap-frog. – Another day the English Ambassador was sitting opposite the King at dinner. His Majesty asked him to take wine. The glasses were filled. The Ambassador bowed and put the wine to his lips. The King grinned hideously and threw his wine into the face of one of the footmen. The other guests kept the most profound gravity. But the Englishman who had but lately come to Copenhagen, though a practiced diplomatist, could not help giving some signs of astonishment. The King immediately addressed him in French, "Eh – mais, Monsieur L'Envoyé d'Angleterre, qu'avez vous donc? Pourquoi riez vous? Est-ce qu'il y ait quelque chose qui vous ait diverti. Faites moi le plaisir de me l'indiquer. J'aime beaucoup les ridicules."

The behaviour of Randolph Churchill, son of Sir Winston and himself an M.P., was notorious throughout his life. Evelyn Waugh, on active service with him in Italy in 1944, recorded that on Tuesday 29th August

RANDOLPH and I drove in a jeep to Naples through a devastated countryside. At Cassino there were notices everywhere forbidding traffic to stop. Here we stopped while Randolph made water before a group of women. When asked why he chose this place he said, "Because I am a member of parliament."

BAD BEHAVIOUR

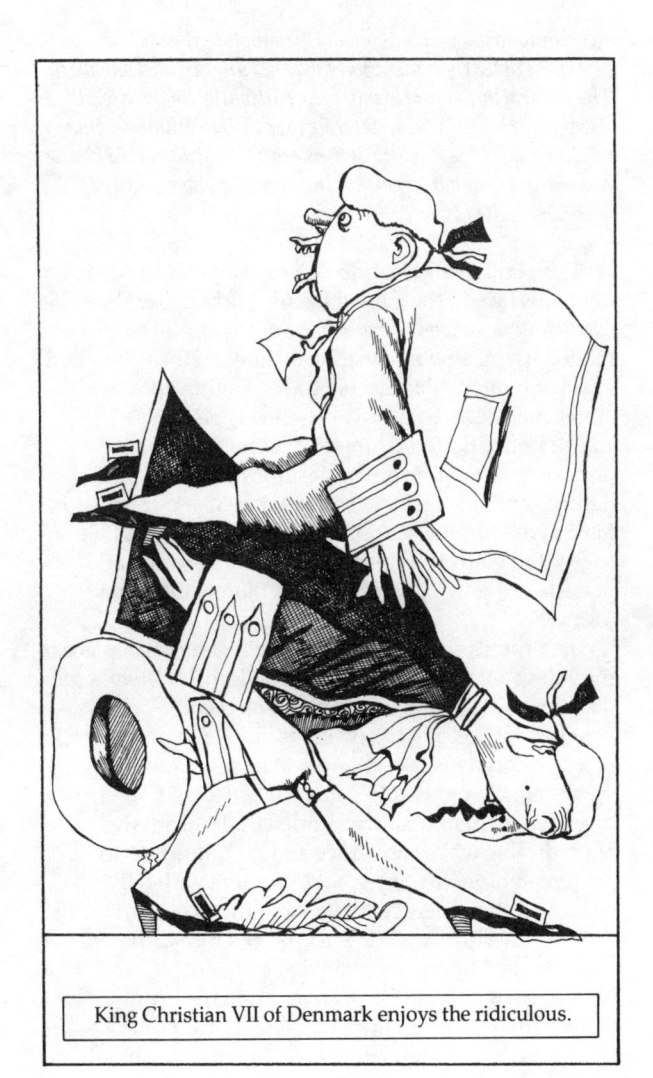

King Christian VII of Denmark enjoys the ridiculous.

Bad Behaviour

According to his great-nephew Christopher, the overriding weakness of Christopher Sykes was his unredeemed snobbery. The natural outlet for this was the cultivation of his friendhsip with the Prince of Wales (later Edward VII) – whatever that might entail. One evening at dinner the Prince, 'moved by heaven knows what joyous whim', tipped a glass of brandy over Sykes's head.

WHEN the brandy landed on his hair and trickled down his face to the golden beard, Christopher showed a rare thing: an excess of presence of mind. Not a muscle moved. Then, after a pause, he inclined to the Prince and said without any discernible trace of annoyance or amusement: "As Your Royal Highness pleases." ...

The Prince flattered himself that he had made a discovery. Always an enthusiast for comedy, he had lighted upon the greatest comic act of his time: to heap farce and buffoonery upon the Antonine figure of his friend and enjoy the contrast between clowning and persistent dignity, here was an absolutely infallible formula...

The Prince's simple taste liked enlargement. In place of the glass a full bottle was substituted, and another royal discovery was that even funnier effects could be conjured by pouring the precious liquid not on to his hair, but down his friend's neck. Amid screams of sycophantic laughter the Prince invented an entirely new diversion. Christopher was hurled underneath the billiard-table while the Prince and his faithful courtiers prevented his escape by spearing at him with billiard-cues. And there were further elaborations of the sousing theme. Watering cans were introduced into Christopher's bedroom and his couch sprinkled by the royal hand. New parlour games were evolved from the Prince's simple but inventive mind: while smoking a cigar he would invite Christopher to gaze into his eyes in order to see the smoke coming out of them, and while Christopher was thus obediently engaged, the Prince would thrust the burning end on to his friend's unguarded hand. And the basis of the joke never weakened. To pour brandy down the neck of some roaring drunken sot of a courtier was one thing; but Christopher remained the statuesque figure he had been on the great night of the brandy glass. He never failed his audience. Never. His hat would be knocked off, the cigar would be applied, the soda-water pumped over his head, and he would incline, and murmur: "As Your Royal Highness pleases."

Even this catalogue does not exhaust the humiliations suffered by the hapless Sykes. For example:

At a ball which the Prince gave at Gunton on 10 January, 1870, it is on record that his friend, Christopher Sykes, became so drunk that he collapsed and had to be put to bed, and that his host retaliated by ordering that a dead sea-gull should be laid beside him. The joke answered so well that a live trussed rabbit was substituted on the following night.

Saint-Simon recorded in his MÉMOIRES *the death in 1699 of the Chevalier de Coislin, brother of the Bishop of Orleans and the Duc de Coislin:*

One story will tell you the whole of him. It happened that he went with his brothers and a fourth (I know not whom) on one of the King's excursions, for he followed the King everywhere, although he would not see him, in order to be with his brothers and their friends. Now the Duc de Coislin was devastatingly polite, so much so that people became bored to tears in his company. He had a habit, when on these journeys, of making endless flowery speeches to the people with whom he lodged, while the chevalier nearly exploded with impatience. On this occasion, they were assigned rooms in the house of a certain gentlewoman, who was lively, well bred, and handsome. There were long civilities in the evening, and still longer speeches next morning. M. d'Orléans, who was not then a cardinal, implored his brother to have done; the chevalier raged; the duke continued to pay his compliments. Coislin, knowing his brother and guessing that there would be no sudden end to the business, decided to relieve himself and wreak his revenge very prettily at the same time.

Later, when they were some ten miles upon their journey, he began to speak of their charming hostess and of all his brother's compliments; then, overcome by laughter, he told the coach party that he had a notion the lady would not feel gratified for long. There was the Duc de Coislin, much puzzled, unable to imagine why, and anxiously asking questions. "Do you really want an answer?" said the chevalier brutally. "Your fine speeches drove me past all bearing, so I went up into the room where you slept and planted an enormous stool plumb in the middle of the floor. At this precise moment, our lovely hostess is in no doubt but that it was you with all your fine compliments who left her that token." ...

They told the story to their friends that evening. It made one of the pleasantest tales of those journeys. To those who knew them, it was the best of all.

*After Duff Cooper ceased to be British Ambassador in Paris in
1947, he and his wife Diana, after the briefest of returns to
England, took up residence at Chantilly, just outside Paris.
As Diana Cooper's biographer records, relations between the
Coopers and their successors, Sir Oliver and Lady Harvey,
soon became strained:*

From a few days after her return to Paris Diana began
to conduct raids on the Embassy to collect items of
furniture which she claimed belonged to her. Lady
Harvey would notice a chair or chandelier had vanished,
ask where it was and be told that Lady Diana had called
for it that morning. Then came the day of the Harveys'
first grand luncheon-party. Diana chanced to call at a
quarter to one in search of more of her possessions. The
guests arrived to find her in the hall. "*Chère Diane!* How
lovely to see you here. We didn't know you were coming
to lunch." "Oh *I'm* not invited. We never are. You'll find
the Harveys up there somewhere," with a gesture
upstairs. The guests clustered around her while upstairs
the Harveys waited and wondered.

---

*From the account of Nell Gwyn, one of the many mistresses of
King Charles II, in Capt. Alexander Smith's* THE SCHOOL OF
VENUS – A HISTORY OF CUCKOLDS AND CUCKOLD-MAKERS,
published in 1716:

She had made many Enemies who envy'd her the
Preferment of being the King's Concubine, as *Barbarah
Villiars* Dutchess of *Cleveland*, *Louise de Querouaille*
Dutchess of *Portsmouth*, and Miss *Davis*. However, *Nell*
neither fear'd 'em nor lov'd 'em; stood her Ground at all
Times, and never affronted any of her Partners in
Iniquity, who would often Complain thereof to the King,

Bad Behaviour

A coup de soleil reduces the mistress of the house to ashes.

but always came off with flying Colours. Once falling out with the Dutchess of *Portsmouth*, in a Scuffle betwixt 'em, *Nell* having *Squintabella* on the Floor, (her Grace being so call'd from a Cast which she had in her Eyes) and taking up her Coats, she burnt with a Candle all the Hair off those Parts which Modesty obliges to Conceal...

Another Time *Nell Gwin* having Notice that Miss *Davis* was to be entertain'd at Night, by the King in his Bed-Chamber, she invited the Lady to a Collation of Sweetmeats, which being made up with physical [i.e. medicinal] Ingredients, the Effects thereof had such an Operation upon the Harlot, when the King was Caressing her in Bed with the amorous Sports of *Venus*, that a violent and sudden Loosness obliging her Ladyship to discharge her Artillery, she made the King, as well as her self, in a most lamentable Pickle; which caused her Royal Master to turn her off, with the small Pension of a Thousand Pounds *per Annum*, in consideration for her former Services, in the Affairs of Love; after which she never appear'd again at Court.

In the Rev. Alexander Dyce's RECOLLECTIONS OF THE TABLE-TALK OF SAMUEL ROGERS *there is attributed to Vernon:*

THE story about the lady being pulverised in India by a *coup de soleil*:– when he was dining there with a Hindoo, one of his host's wives was suddenly reduced to ashes; upon which, the Hindoo *rang the bell*, and said to the attendant who answered it, "Bring fresh glasses, and sweep up your mistress."

Augustus Hare records in his journal the reminiscences of an old friend, the Hon. Augusta Barrington:

"GEORGE IV., as Prince Regent, was very charming when he was not drunk, but he generally *was*. Do you remember how he asked Curran to dinner to amuse him – only for that? Curran was up to it, and sat silent all through dinner. This irritated the Prince, and at last, after dinner, when he had had a good deal too much, he filled a glass with wine and threw it in Curran's face, with 'Say something funny, can't you!' Curran, without moving a muscle, threw his own glass of wine in his neighbour's face, saying, 'Pass his Royal Highness's joke.'"

Osbert Sitwell remembers his first leave from the horrors of the Western Front in 1915:

WHEN I arrived from Flanders, I was put in a bedroom on the ground floor, but entirely cut off from the rest of the house. It was dark and inconvenient, and I slept badly in it. I asked if I could be moved. My father, however, had read in the papers that the troops in the trenches were infested with lice, and he now explained to me that he had selected a room far away on purpose, in case I was acting as host to a pack of these vermin, since the distance made it less likely that they would attack him – for if they did, it might, he pointed out, entail very serious consequences! When I became angry, for personal cleanliness has always been something of an obsession with me, and protested that if thus afflicted I should not go to stay in any house and that it was a slur on me to suggest it, he fluttered his hand at me condescendingly, and replied, "Not at all, my dear boy. It's no disgrace. Any primitive form of life is most interesting!"

BAD BEHAVIOUR

From Henry Crabb Robinson's diary, February 21st., 1838:

I spent a couple of hours with Mr. George Young. I took courage to relate to him an anecdote about himself. Nearly forty years ago, I happened to be in a Hackney stage-coach with Young. A stranger came in – it was opposite Lackington's. On a sudden the stranger struck Young a violent blow on the face. Young coolly put his head out of the window and told the coachman to let him out. Not a word passed between the stranger and Young. But the latter having alighted, said in a calm voice, before he shut the door, "Ladies and gentlemen, that is my father."

The well-honed collector's instinct of Queen Mary, wife of George V, was notorious. When, towards the end of her life, there came into her possession a Russian ikon of great beauty but unknown origin, the most strenuous efforts were made to establish its provenance, to no avail.

THEN someone in her Household recollected that there was a Russian princess – a cousin of the British Royal Family – still living in the London suburb whither she had fled to escape the Bolsheviks in 1917. Possibly she would know something about the ikon. Queen Mary concurred and at once wrote to the Princess, inviting her to tea.

The Princess, who had lived 30 years in poverty and obscurity, resigned to the ostracism of her Windsor cousins, was overjoyed. Her joy increased at the tea party, as Queen Mary spoke to her kindly about her parents and relations and the dear dead days under the Tsar. At long last, her wanderings and loneliness seemed to have come to an end. Then Queen Mary brought out the ikon and asked if she knew anything about it.

The Princess took the ikon and pressed it to her heart. She did, indeed, know something about it. She said it was the very ikon given to her at her baptism – the ikon which hung over her bed through her early childhood and to which, each night, she had said her prayers. It was the ikon to which she had prayed for deliverance on the night the Bolsheviks broke into her house, killing her father and mother, her brothers and sisters. It was the ikon she had gone back into the blazing house to rescue, and had carried with her through her long years as a refugee, her sole source of beauty and inspiration until hunger and cold had at last forced her to sell it for a few pennies. Even now, in her illness and despair, its sacred, fragile loveliness still haunted her dreams. The ikon had saved her life. The ikon *was* her life.

"I see," Queen Mary said, taking the ikon smartly back. "Thank you *so* much for identifying it."

Posterity owes to Samuel Burdy's THE LIFE OF THE LATE REV. PHILIP SKELTON, *published in 1792, this account of one Dr. Madden, 'a gentleman greatly esteemed in those times':*

THE Doctor, as well as our great countryman, had a real regard for Ireland, and strove, as it appears, according to his abilities, to serve it. It being customary for him to go among the nobility and gentry soliciting subscriptions for useful purposes, he met with an odd reception in Dublin on an errand of this sort (as Mr. Skelton informed us) from a late nobleman, a famous member of the hell-fire club. His Lordship, on being told that the Doctor was in the parlour, shrewdly guessing at his business, immediately stript himself stark naked, and in this state, came running into the room with out-

Bad Behaviour

Dr Madden is shown the door.

stretched arms, saying, "worthy Dr. Madden, I am glad to see you, how do you do? shake hands with me Doctor, when I heard you were here, I was in such a hurry to see you, that I would not wait to put on my clothes." The Doctor shocked at the wild spectacle, leaped up, and was for hastening out of the room; but his Lordship stopped him saying, "my dear Doctor, don't be in a hurry, tell me your business, I would be glad to do any thing to serve you." The Doctor pushed past him, but his Lordship accompanied him to the street door, where he stood for some time as a *show* to the people passing by.

In his REMINISCENCES, *published in 1828, Henry Angelo provided an exhaustive catalogue of the society figures of his day, among them the Duke of Norfolk:*

THE duke, long addicted to self-indulgence, had an extensive and increasing list of annuities to pay to women of various grades, as the wages of their shame. It was said, that these were paid quarterly, at a certain banker's; the checks being drawn payable on a certain day, to all the parties. Such frail pensioners were not likely to postpone their receipts; and aware of this, the duke used to sit in a back parlour, to have a peep at his old acquaintances, the name of whom as each applied, he knew, as a clerk was appointed to bring the cheque as presented, for the duke's inspection. There he would make his comments to a confidential person, at his elbow. Of one he would say, "I'faith, she looks as young as twenty years ago." Of another, "What a dowdy!" and of another, "What an old hag!" Occasionally, however, a feeling of compunction, or perhaps of caprice, would seize him, when he would desire the party to step in, and there, after inquiring of their welfare, strange to say, he would sometimes entertain them with a gratuitous lecture on morality.

BAD BEHAVIOUR

Not only the former mistresses were numerous.
It is recorded that

DRIVING through the village of Greystoke in Cumberland with his steward, he saw hordes of children waving at them from both sides of the road. "Whose are all those children?" he asked. The steward answered, "Some are mine, Your Grace, and some are yours."

Extracts from an unpublished diary of Lord Robert Seymour,
M.P. and man of fashion, 1788:

AT Mrs. Vaneck's assembly last week, the Prince of Wales, very much to the honor of his polite and elegant Behaviour, measured the breadth of Mrs. V. behind with his Handkerchief, and shew'd the measurement to most of the Company.

The P. of W. called on Miss Vaneck last week with two of his Equerries. On coming into the Room he exclaimed, "I *must* do it; I *must* do it." Miss V. asked him what it was that he was obliged to do, when he winked at St. Leger and the other *accomplice,* who lay'd Miss V. on the Floor, and the P. possitively wipped her. The occasion of this extraordinary behaviour was occasioned by a Bett wch. I suppose he had made in one of his mad Fits. The next day, however, he wrote her a penitential Letter, and she now receives him on the same footing as ever.

The Prince of Wales very much affronted the D. of Orleans and his natural Brother, L'Abbé de la Fai, at Newmarket, L'Abbé declaring it possible to charm a Fish out of the Water, which being disputed occasioned a Bett; and the Abbé stooped down over the water to tickle the Fish with a little switch. Fearing, however, the Prince sd.

play him some Trick, he declared he hoped the P. wd. not use him unfairly by throwing him into the water. The P. answer'd him that he wd. not upon his Honor. The Abbé had no sooner begun the operation by leaning over a little Bridge when the P. took hold of his heels and threw him into the Water, which was rather deep...

Prince of Wales, Mrs. FitzHerbert, the Duke and Dutchess of Cumberland, and Miss Pigott, Mrs. F.'s companion, went a Party to Windsor during the absence of *The Family* fm. Windsor; and going to see a cold Bath Miss P. expressed a great wish to bathe this hot weather. The D. of C. very imprudently pushed her in, and the Dut. of C. having the presence of mind to throw out the Rope saved her when in such a disagreeable State from fear and surprise as to be near sinking. Mrs. F. went into convulsion Fits, and the Dut. fainted away, and the scene proved ridiculous in the extreme, as Report says the Duke called out to Miss P. that he was instantly coming to her in the water, and continued undressing himself. Poor Miss P.'s clothes entirely laid upon the water, and made her appear an awkward figure. They afterwards pushed in one of the Prince's attendants.

From Augustus Hare's journal, 4 June, 1882:

TALK of strange relics led to mention of the heart of a French king preserved at Nuneham in a silver casket. Dr. Buckland, whilst looking at it, exclaimed, "I have eaten many strange things, but have never eaten the heart of a king before," and, before any one could hinder him, he had gobbled it up, and the precious relic was lost for ever.

Bad Behaviour

Dr Buckland consumes his first royal heart.

Among the 'irregular notes' kept by Evelyn Waugh instead of a diary towards the end of his life was this reminiscence of the Countess of Rosse:

TUGBOAT Annie Rosse, being conducted round the estate at Birr, was taken to a turf cabin where a crone sat in pig dung smoking a pipe and complaining of the roof. "My dear, don't change a thing. It's simply *you*!"

From Lord Glenbervie's diary, October 29, 1796:

LORD Thanet had invited several of his country neighbours to dine with him and had entreated of Lady Thanet that she would treat them with civility, which she promised to do. When they were assembled, she came into the drawing room and after the common bows and curtsies, she said, "Gentlemen, I beg you will be on no ceremony here – do exactly as if you were at home – get upon all fours."

Thomas, Earl of Ailesbury described in his MEMOIRS *how the boorishness of the Duke of Lauderdale finally became insupportable to Charles II and his Court:*

THE king did some of his court honour to dine or sup with them, and a select company, agreeable to his pleasant and witty humour. This lord, although not invited, ever intruded himself. A Courtier Lord, or other whose name I have forgot, desired of the king to do him that honour, which he accepted, "but" said he "we shall be pestered with such a one." The inviter replied "If your majesty will give way to it, I have invented a means to disgust him so at my house that your majesty, no doubt, for ever after will be freed from him." That person ordered a double sillibub glass, and it was concerted that the king, after having drunk plentifully, should ask the master of the house for a sillibub to refresh him; and by a token the king knew which of the two to take, and commending it greatly, the Duke Lauderdale, for such was his title then, took the double glass in his hand, he having a great share of confidence (very natural to one of his country) and drinking the other half which was prepared with horse urine, swore that no person had such a taste as his majesty. In some little time it worked as it was natural, and the king perceiving it, cried out, "My lord Lauderdale is sick," and they carried him away, and the king was never troubled more with him on such diverting occasions.

In his autobiography, ANOTHER SELF, *James Lees-Milne describes the hostility between his father and the local vicar, so intense that every service was a pitched battle between them. Lees-Milne possessed one formidable weapon: the choice of lesson was his alone, and when reading it he was able to give the vicar as good as he got.*

ON one occasion in a particularly vindictive mood he announced: "Here beginneth the 36th chapter of the Book of Genesis, verses 1 to 43."

After fixing the Vicar in his turn with a steely eye, he started off: "Now these are the generations of Esau, who is Edom. Esau took his wives of the daughters of Canaan; Adah the daughter of Elon the Hittite, and

Aholibamah the daughter of Annah the daughter of Zibeon the Hivite; and Bashemath Ismael's daughter, sister of Nebajoth. And Adah bare to Esau, Eliphaz: and Bashemath bare Reuel." On and on he droned. This was what he called enjoying his pound of flesh. First the farmers' wives, then Miss Empey, although so devout, then the schoolmistress dropped off, and last of all the servants from the manor at the risk of a severe reprimand after the service. Not so the Vicar. He shifted, took off his pince-nez, cleared his throat, and puffed out his cheeks to no avail. My father relentlessly continued. "And the sons of Eliphaz were Teman, Omah, Zepho, and Gatam, and Kenaz. And Timna was concubine to Eliphaz, Esau's son. And these are the sons of Reuel; Nahath, and Zerah, Shammah and Mizzah..." The Vicar becoming desperate made a sign for help to my mother who up to now had been remarkably patient. She nodded assent, and in her turn made signs to my father to stop. He took no notice and went on: "And the children of Ezer are these; Bilhan, and Zaavan, and Achan; and of Dishan, Uz and Fuz. These are the dukes that came of the Horites; Duke Lotan, Duke Shobal, Duke Zibeon, Duke Anah."

My mother could bear it no longer. She half rose in her seat, and making a face of pained embarrassment, mouthed the words, "Your buttons!" while nodding a downward glance at my father's trousers. Instantly he turned scarlet, slid a hand across his stomach, and abruptly halted at the words, "And the name of the city was Pau." Mumbling, "Here endeth the first lesson," he sidled back into the pew. My mother was triumphant. She nudged him in the ribs and said, "April fool!" My father looked perplexed. "But it isn't April," he retorted. "It's August."

According to his obituary in the GENTLEMAN'S MAGAZINE *for October 1789, James Hamilton, 8th Earl of Abercorn, was 'highly offended if any person presumed to visit him without the formality of a card of invitation.'*

Dr. Robertson, the celebrated historian, not aware of this, went to pay his respects to the noble Earl, and found him walking in a shrubbery which had been lately planted. The Doctor, wishing to pay a compliment to the soil, observed the shrubs had grown considerably since his Lordship's last visit; "They have nothing else to do," replied his Lordship; and immediately turning on his heel, left the Doctor without uttering another word.

The American hostess Lulie Dearbergh was famous in Florence for the ribaldry of her conversation; according to Harold Acton, her 'dinners were as formal as her talk was loose.' Max Beerbohm dined with her only once, as he later recalled to Reggie Turner:

The dinner, I remember, was very good. But I felt, as I sat listening to my hostess's conversation, that I was having a beautiful dinner in a cesspool. The well-trained English butler, noticing me grow paler and paler – and knowing, by his experience of other *débutants* at his mistress's table, what was going to happen – placed beside my plate a large and priceless majolica basin. The first time I was sick into it I apologised elaborately to Mrs Deerburg. She made very light of the matter. "You'll be worse," she said, "before you're better," and resumed the thread of her conversation.

Walter Savage Landor damages the violets.

After the death of her first husband, Mrs Dearbergh married the Marchese Carlo Torrigiani. As Harold Acton confirms, however, her style remained unaltered:

ON one occasion a retired diplomat who had been arrested for indecent behaviour in the Cascine was asked to turn round. "I want to see if you wear a zipper behind", said the Marchesa.

In his memoir of the 19th-century writer Walter Savage Landor, Lord Houghton emphasised the author's sentimental love of flowers:

IN his garden he would bend over the flowers with a sort of worship, but rarely touched one of them...

The form which the notoriety of this sentiment took in the Florentine legend was that he had one day, after an imperfect dinner, thrown the cook out of the window, and, while the man was writhing with a broken limb, ejaculated, "Good God! I forgot the violets."

From Lord Glenbervie's diary, December 16, 1793:

LORD Pembroke had an only daughter of whom he was very fond. She died when she was about ten or eleven years of age, and the very next day a person of the family who happened to go into the father's room found on his table, in his own hand, a calculation of how much he would save by her death.

BAD BEHAVIOUR

Ernest Hemingway's behaviour while courting his fourth wife, Mary, in Paris in 1944 goes a long way to explaining the failure of his three previous marriages: according to his latest biographer, Hemingway

PLACED a photograph of her Australian husband in the toilet bowl, blasted it with a machine pistol and flooded their room at the Ritz.

The weapon, captured from a German officer, had just been given to Hemingway by his friend Colonel Buck Lanham. The gunman's speech to the hotel management, who came running to the scene, is recorded by Carlos Baker:

HE took his stand on the bidet like a Fourth of July orator. *"Messieurs,"* he said, *"je regrette profondément le malheureux incident. Messieurs, permettez-moi de vous présenter mon ami, le Colonel Lanham, qui sera bientôt général. C'est un soldat de ligne formidable qui a été sous le feu de l'ennemi sans arrêt depuis les débarquements de Normandie, et n'a eu depuis repos ni distractions. Il est venu ici pour nous rendre visite, à Madame et moi-même. Il nous a dit qu'il désirait utiliser les toilettes. Quand il s'assit pour se soulager, Boum!...Et vous pouvez vous-mêmes, Messieurs, vous rendre compte des résultats. Nous n'avons plus de temps à perdre. Il me faut une nouvelle toilette immédiatement, avant le matin."*

Bad Behaviour

Hemingway damages a Paris bathroom.

From Dr. Thomas Birch's description of the feasts given by his contemporary, Peter the Great of Russia:

THEY often tie eight or ten young mice on a string, & hide them under green pease, or in such Soups as the Russians have the greatest appetite for; which sets them a kicking & vomiting in a most beastly manner, when they come to the bottom, & discover the Trick. They often bake Cats, Wolves, Ravens, & the like in their pastries; & when the Company have eat them up, they tell them what stuff they have in their Guts.

The present Butler is one of the Czar's Buffoons, to whom he has given the name of *Witasihi*, with this privilege, that if anybody else calls him by that Name, he has Leave to drub him with his wooden sword. If therefore anybody upon the Czar's setting them on calls out *Witasihi*, & the fellow does not know exactly, who it was, he falls a beating them all round, beginning with Prince Mentzicoff, & ending with the last of the Company, without excepting even the Ladies, whom he strips of their head-clothes, as he does the old Russians of their Wigs, which he tramples upon. On which Occasion it is pleasant enough to see the Variety of their bald pates.

In his TRADITIONS OF EDINBURGH, *published in 1825, Robert Chambers gave a vivid portrait of Catherine Hyde, Duchess of Queensberry:*

SHE was, in reality, insane, though the politeness of fashionable society, and the flattery of her poetical friends, seem rather to have attributed her extravagances to an agreeable freedom of carriage and vivacity of mind.

When in Scotland, her Grace always dressed herself in the garb of a peasant girl. This she seems to have done, in order to ridicule and put out of countenance the stately dresses and demeanour of the Scottish gentlewomen who visited her. One evening, some country ladies paid her a visit, dressed in their best brocades, as for some state occasion. Her Grace proposed a walk, and they were of course under the disagreeable necessity of trooping off in all the splendour of full dress, to the utter discomfiture of their starched-up frills and flounces. Her Grace, at last, pretending to be tired, sat down upon the dirtiest dunghill she could find, at the end of a farm-house, and saying – "Pray, ladies, be seated," invited the poor draggled fine ladies to seat themselves around her. They stood so much in awe of her, that they durst not refuse; and, of course, her Grace had the exquisite satisfaction of spoiling all their silks...

When she went out to an evening-entertainment, and found a tea-equipage paraded which she thought too fine for the rank of the owner, she would contrive to overset the table, and break the china. The forced politeness of her hosts on such occasions, and the assurances which they made her Grace that no harm was done, &c., delighted her exceedingly.

From THE OLIO, *a collection of essays and anecdotes by the antiquary Francis Grose, published posthumously in 1793:*

THE Rev. Mr. Patten, curate of Whitstable, was of a very singular character: he had originally been a sea chaplain, and contracted much of the tar-like roughness: he was of an athletic make, and had some wit and humour, not restrained by any very strict ideas of professional propriety. He was for many years curate of Whitstable, at a very small stipend, and used to travel, to serve that and another church, in a butcher's cart. Whitstable is situated by the sea-side, and is extremely agueish; so that had he been dismissed, it would not have been easy for the Archbishop of Canterbury, who was the rector, to have procured another curate at the same price. This he well knew; and, presuming on it, was a terror to every new Archbishop.

Mr. Patten was not a rigid high priest; he openly kept a mistress; and on any one going into church in sermon time, and shewing him a lemon, he would instantly conclude his discourse and adjoin to the alehouse...

[He] long refused to read the Athanasian Creed. The Archdeacon, reproving him for that omission, told him, his Grace the Archbishop read it: that may be, answered Patten, perhaps he may believe it, but I don't: he believes at the rate of seven thousand per annum; I at that of less than fifty.

Augustus Hare was invited in July 1889 to meet the Shah of Persia, Nasr-ed-Din, at Hatfield House, home of the Prime Minister, Lord Salisbury:

He is a true Eastern potentate in his consideration for himself and himself only: is most unconcernedly late whenever he chooses: utterly ignores every one he does not want to speak to: amuses himself with monkeyish and often dirty tricks: sacrifices a cock to the rising sun, and wipes his wet hands on the coat-tails of the gentleman next to him without compunction. He expressed his wonder that Lord Salisbury did not take a new wife, though he gave Lady Salisbury a magnificent jewelled order. He knows no English and very few words of French, but when the Baroness Coutts, as the great benefactress of her country, was presented to him by the Prince of Wales, he looked in her face and exclaimed, "Quelle horreur!"

Evelyn Waugh, serving as a Marine in 1940, writes home to his wife:

YESTERDAY was an alarming day. The Brigadier suddenly accosted Messer-Bennets & me & said, "I hear you are staying in camp for the week-end. You will spend the day with me." So at 12.30 he picked us up in his motor-car and drove all over the road to his house which was the lowest type of stockbroker's Tudor and I said in a jaggering way "Did you build this house, sir?" and he said "Build it! It's 400 years old!" The Brigadier's madam is kept very much in her place and ordered about with great shouts "Woman, go up to my cabin and get my boots". More peculiar, she is subject to booby-traps. He told us with great relish how the night before she had had to get up several times in the night to look after a daughter who was ill and how, each time she returned, he had fixed up some new horror to injure her – a string across the door, a jug of water on top of it etc. However she seemed to thrive on this treatment & was very healthy & bright with countless children.

So after luncheon we were taken for a walk with the Brigadier who kept saying "Don't call me 'sir'." He told us how when he had a disciplinary case he always said, "Will you be court martialled or take it from me". The men said, "Take it from you, sir", so "I bend 'em over and give 'em ten of the best with a cane." ...

He said, "There's only one man in Egypt you can trust. Hassanin Bey. Luckily he's chief advisor to the King. He is a white man. I'll tell you something that'll show you the kind of chap he is. He and I were alone in a carriage going from Luxor to Suez – narrow gauge, single track line, desert on both sides, blazing heat. Ten hours with nothing to do. I thought I should go mad. Luckily I had a golf ball with me. So I made Hassanin stand one end of the corridor and we threw that ball backwards & forwards as hard as we could the whole day – threw it so that it really hurt. Not many Gyppies would stand up to that. Ever since then I've known there was at least one Gyppy we could trust."

Robert, Lord Lytton, Viceroy of India, describes in a letter to a friend the visit to Calcutta in 1880 of the former President of the United States, Ulysses S. Grant:

On their last night at Calcutta General Grant and 'Suite' – with the exception of Mrs G (who was 'incommoded in her inside') dined with the Chief Justice Sir R. Garth and Lady Garth, from whose house they embarked. On this occasion 'our distinguished guest' the double Ex-President of the 'Great Western Republic', who got as drunk as a fiddle, showed that he could also be as profligate as a lord. He fumbled Mrs A., kissed the shrieking Miss B. – pinched the plump Mrs C. black and blue – and ran at Miss D. with intent to ravish her.

Finally, after throwing all the Garths' female guests into hysterics by generally behaving like a mûst elephant, the noble beast was captured by main force and carried (quatre pattes dans l'air) by six sailors on board the ship which relieved India of his distinguished presence. The marine officer who superintended the carriage of the General from the house to the ship, reports that, when deposited in the public saloon cabin, where Mrs G. was awaiting him with her cock in her eye, this remarkable man satiated there and then his baffled lust on the unresisting body of his legitimate spouse, and copiously vomited during the operation. If you have seen Mrs Grant you will not think this incredible.

Frances Partridge noted in her diary a story she heard about the writer Simon Raven and his ex-wife:

AFTER he had broken with her she telegraphed: "Wife and baby starving". Simon is supposed to have wired back: "Eat baby".

SOURCES QUOTED IN THE TEXT

Acton, Harold, *More Memoirs of an Aesthete*, Methuen, 1970
Ailesbury, Thomas, Earl of, *Memoirs*, ed. W.E. Buckley, Roxburghe Club, 1890
Ainslie, Douglas, *Adventures Social and Literary*, T. Fisher Unwin, 1922
Angelo, Henry, *Reminiscences*, Henry Colburn, 1828
Aubrey, John, *Brief Lives*, ed. Oliver Dawson Dick, Secker and Warburg, 1949
Baker, Carlos, *Ernest Hemingway*, Macmillan, 1986
Barker, E.H., *Literary Anecdotes and Contemporary Reminiscences*, J.R. Smith, 1852
Beaton, Cecil, *The Strenuous Years*, Weidenfeld and Nicolson, 1973
Beerbohm, Max, *Letters to Reggie Turner*, ed. Rupert Hart-Davis, Rupert Hart-Davis, 1964
Boswell, James, *The Life of Samuel Johnson*, Charles Dilly, 1791
Brinnin, John Malcolm, *Truman Capote: A Memoir*, Sidgwick & Jackson, 1987
British Museum, Add. MSS 4164
British Museum, Ashley MSS 5753
Burdy, Samuel, *The Life of the late Rev. Philip Skelton*, 1792
Byron, Lord, *Works*, ed. Ernest Hartley Coleridge, John Murray, 1898
Caufield, Catherine, *The Emperor of the United States of America and other magnificent British eccentrics*, Routledge & Kegan Paul, 1981
Chambers, Robert, *Traditions of Edinburgh*, W.& C. Tait, 1825
Delany, Paul, *The Neo-Pagans*, Macmillan, 1987
Douglas, Sylvester, Lord Glenbervie, *Diaries*, ed. Francis Bickley, Constable, 1928
Eynsham, Adam of, *Magna Vita Sancti Hugonis*, ed. & tr. Decima L. Douie and David Hugh Farmer, Clarendon Press, 1981
Fielding, Daphne, *Mercury Presides*, Eyre & Spottiswoode, 1954
Fleming, Ann, *Letters*, ed. Mark Amory, Collins, 1985
Fowler, Gene, *Good Night, Sweet Prince*, Hammond, Hammond, 1949
Fox, Henry Edward, *Journal*, ed. Earl of Ilchester, Thornton Butterworth, 1923
Fox, James, *White Mischief*, Jonathan Cape, 1982
Fraser, Sir William, *Hic et Ubique*, Sampson, Low, 1893
The Gentlemen's Magazine, October 1789
Grose, Francis, *The Olio*, S. Hooper, 1793
Hamilton, Anthony, *Memoirs of the life of Count de Grammont*, tr. A. Boyer, 1714
Hare, A.J.C., *The Story of My Life*, George Allen, 1896
Harington, Sir John, *Nugae Antiquae*, ed. Henry Harington, W. Frederick, 1769
Harpsfield, Nicholas, *A Treatise on the Pretended Divorce between Henry VIII. and Catharine of Aragon*, Camden Society, vol. NS XXI, 1878
Herbert, Dorothea, *Retrospections*, Gerald Howe, 1929
Hervey, Lord, *Memoirs*, ed. Romney Sedgewick, William Kimber, 1952

Hibbert, Christopher, *Edward VII: A Portrait*, Allen Lane, 1976
Hibbert, Christopher, *George IV, Prince of Wales*, Longmans, 1972
Houghton, Lord, *Monographs*, 1873
Lake, Dr. Edward, *Diary*, ed. G.P. Elliot, The Camden Miscellany, vol. I, 1847
Lees-Milne, James, *Another Self*, Hamish Hamilton, 1970
Lejeune, Anthony, *The Gentlemen's Clubs of London*, Macdonald and Jane's, 1979
Leslie, Anita, *Edwardians in Love*, Hutchinson, 1972
Lilly, William, *History of his Life and Times*, J. Roberts, 1715
Lutyens, Mary, *The Lyttons in India*, John Murray, 1979
Magnus, Philip, *King Edward VII*, John Murray, 1964
Malmesbury, Earl of, *Diaries and Correspondence*, ed. Earl of Malmesbury, R. Bentley, 1844
Masters, Brian, *The Dukes*, Blond and Briggs, 1975
Maugham, W. Somerset, *The Vagrant Mood*, Heinemann, 1952
Meyers, Jeffrey, *Hemingway*, Macmillan, 1986
Montagu, Lady Mary Wortley, *Letters*, ed. Robert Halsband, Clarendon Press, 1965
Moore, Thomas, *Memoirs, Journals and Correspondence*, ed. Lord John Russell, 1853
Nevill, Ralph, *Sporting Days and Sporting Ways*, Duckworth, 1910
Newton, Rev. Benjamin, *Diary*, ed. C.P. Fendall and E.A. Crutchley, Cambridge University Press, 1933
Norman, Philip, *Awful Moments*, Elm Tree, 1986
d'Orleans, Charlotte Elizabeth, Duchesse, *Letters from Liselotte*, ed. & tr. Maria Kroll, Victor Gollancz, 1970
Osborne, Charles, *W.H. Auden: The Life of a Poet*, Eyre Methuen, 1980
Osborne, John, *A Better Class of Person*, Faber & Faber, 1981
The Oxford Chronicle, 7 October 1893
Parsons, Robert, *A Treatise of Three Conversions of England from Paganisme to Christian Religion*, 1603
Partridge, Burgo, *A History of Orgies*, Anthony Blond, 1958
Partridge, Frances, *Everything to Lose*, Victor Gollancz, 1985
Pepys, Samuel, *Diary*, ed. Robert Latham and William Matthews, G. Bell, 1971
Robinson, Henry Crabb, *Diary, Reminiscences, Correspondence*, ed. Thomas Sadler, 1869
Rogers, Samuel, *Recollections of the Table-Talk of Samuel Rogers*, ed. Alexander Dyce, 1856
Russell, G.W.E., *Collections and Recollections*, Smith, Elder, 1898
Saint-Simon, Duc de, *Saint-Simon at the Court of Versailles*, ed. and tr. Lucy Norton, Hamish Hamilton, 1958
Seaman, Barbara, *Lovely Me*, Sidgwick & Jackson, 1988
Sitwell, Edith, *Taken Care Of*, Hutchinson, 1965
Sitwell, Osbert, *Laughter in the Next Room* Macmillan, 1949
Sladen, Douglas, *Twenty Years of My Life*, Constable, 1915
Smith, Alexander, *The School of Venus*, J. Morphew; J. Baker, 1716
Sykes, Christopher, *Four Studies in Loyalty*, Collins, 1946

Taylor, John, *Record of My Life*, Edward Bull, 1832

Thomas, Donald, *Swinburne: The Poet in his World*, Weidenfeld and Nicolson, 1979

Timbs, George, *English Eccentrics and Eccentricities*, 1866

Trevelyan, G.O., *The Life and Letters of Lord Macaulay*, 1876

Turner, E.S., *Amazing Graceu, Michael Joseph*, 1975

Waugh, Evelyn, *Diaries*, ed. Michael Davie, Weidenfeld and Nicolson, 1976

Waugh, Evelyn, *Letters*, ed. Mark Amory, Weidenfeld and Nicolson, 1980

Walpole, Horace, *Letters Addressed to the Countess of Ossory*, ed. R. Vernon Smith, 1848

Walpole, Horace, *Letters to George Montagu*, 1819

Walpole, Horace, *Memoirs of the Reign of George III*, ed. Sir Denis le Marchant, 1845

Wilde, Oscar, *Intentions*, Heinemann & Balestier, 1891

Wood, Anthony, *Life and Times*, ed. Andrew Clark, Oxford Historical Society, 1892

Woodcock, Thomas, *Papers*, ed. G.C. Moore Smith, The Camden Miscellany, vol. XI. 1907

Ziegler, Philip, *Diana Cooper*, Hamish Hamilton, 1981